COMPLETE

ATHLETE

...

UNDERSTANDING
THE JOURNEY
TO BECOMING A TRUE
PROFESSIONAL

ISBN-978-0-9990217-2-9

Printed in the United States of America.

At the time of this book's publication, all facts and figures cited are the most current available. All telephone numbers, addresses, and website URLs are accurate and active. All publications, organizations, websites, and other resources exist as described in the book, and all have been verified. The authors and Publisher/ Complete Athlete, LLC make no warranty or guarantee concerning the information and materials given out by organizations or content found at websites, and we are not responsible for any changes that occur after this book's publication. If you find an error, please contact Complete Athlete, LLC.

Complete Athlete, LLC
660 Newport Center Drive
Suite 200
Newport Beach, CA 92660
Phone: (714) 949-3845
www.mycompleteathlete.com

To all of you who allow yourselves to believe something inside you is superior to circumstance, who allow yourselves to dream fearlessly, and who are constantly striving to become the best version of yourself—this book is for you.

TABLE OF CONTENTS

INTRODUCTION

**EVER WONDER WHAT IT TRULY TAKES TO
BECOME A PROFESSIONAL ATHLETE?**

Making it to the professional stage in any sport requires heart, determination, grit, resiliency, and tenacity. How many young athletes sit in front of their families' television and watch the Opening Ceremonies for the Olympic Games every four years, dreaming of what it must be like to represent their country on a world stage, visualizing their moment of when they stand atop the podium someday in their future? Athletes who make it to the professional level all have one thing in common: the will to never give in combined with the drive to see every opportunity as a chance to improve.

**BUT WHETHER YOU MAKE IT PROFESSIONALLY
OR NOT, YOU CAN ALWAYS STRIVE TO BECOME
A COMPLETE ATHLETE.**

In athletics, regardless of the sport, we are driven by competition—by the idea that to become better, we must be bigger, stronger, and faster. But did you know those three things actually have nothing to do with becoming a **COMPLETE ATHLETE**? Becoming a **COMPLETE ATHLETE** is about so much more than your skill level or your strength. It is that constant drive to understand, as athletes, our journeys are about so much more than any destination, they are about the individuals we become as a result of those journeys.

This book will challenge you to look at the athletic journey from a different perspective with advice and stories from Paralympic Gold medalist Mallory Weggemann as she intimately discusses overcoming adversity, challenging perception, and pushing the boundaries of possibility.

There are five levels to becoming a **COMPLETE ATHLETE**. Generally speaking, the five levels correspond to the following (although there may be some overlap):

Level 1 - Elementary school athlete
Level 2 - Middle school athlete
Level 3 - High school athlete
Level 4 - College athlete
Level 5 - Professional athlete

A **COMPLETE ATHLETE** must also achieve the highest levels in five different categories:

ATTITUDE is the manner in which you conduct yourself both on and off the field of play. Your attitude has a direct reflection on not only who you are as a person, but also the greater community you represent.

PREPARATION is about more than just showing up to practice each day. Preparation is learning the art of being not just mindful, but also intentional in how you approach your journey to becoming a **COMPLETE ATHLETE**.

FITNESS refers to your physical ability to compete and adapt in your sport as you advance through the stages of your athletic career.

TECHNIQUE refers to your skill level and your ability to continue to learn as you progress as an athlete.

LIFESTYLE is about learning to manage your priorities between your academics, social life, and family. It is also how you live your sport in competition, practice, and daily life.

ATTITUDE	**PREPARATION**	**LIFESTYLE**
Respect	**FITNESS**	Family
Sportsmanship	**TECHNIQUE**	Academics
Teamwork		Social Life
Professionalism		Role Model
Leadership		Living Your Sport

Each category is part of the overall development and character of a **COMPLETE ATHLETE**. "Character," according to Merriam-Webster, is "the way someone thinks, feels, and behaves." All of these aspects influence what kind of person and athlete you are.

If you look at the matrix above, you'll see several categories have attributes that relate to your actions off the field of play. What you do off the field of play affects how you perform on the field of play; for instance, maintaining good fitness will make a big difference in your ability to perform the techniques needed.

The key here is just because someone is a professional athlete in the sense of being paid as an athlete, he or she might not necessarily be considered a professional according to the **COMPLETE ATHLETE** matrix. Becoming a **COMPLETE ATHLETE** is about so much more than your performance—it is about the person you become as a result of your athletic journey.

JOIN THE CONVERSATION!
Find more ways to live a balanced lifestyle in the **COMPLETE ATHLETE** app!

INTRODUCING:
MALLORY WEGGEMANN

Mallory Weggemann started swimming competitively at age 7. In January 2008, she was paralyzed at age 18 after an epidural injection to treat back pain, and she thought her days of swimming were over. After watching the 2008 Paralympic Swimming Trials at the University of Minnesota, she returned to the water in April, less than three months after her injury. She has been swimming ever since.

Weggemann competed in her first international competition in Rio de Janeiro, Brazil, as a member of the United States 2009 IPC Short Course World Championship team. At Worlds, she claimed her first international medals: five golds. She also broke six World Records and seven American Records. Weggemann then competed at the 2010 IPC Swimming Long Course World Championships in the Netherlands, winning eight gold medals and one silver. She broke nine World Records and was recognized as the best performing athlete at Worlds overall. After her performance at the 2010 IPC Long Course World Championships, Weggemann was awarded the 2011 ESPN ESPY Award for Best Female Athlete with a Disability.

Weggemann has represented Team USA at two Paralympic Games. In London 2012, she won both gold and bronze and set a Paralympic Record in 50m Freestyle. She competed in the Rio 2016 Paralympic Games, where she swam all seven individual events and made it into the top 8 in five of the seven. She is currently focused on continuing her career with her eyes set on the Tokyo 2020 Paralympic Games.

When she is not training for competition, Weggemann is a motivational speaker whose audiences range from educational groups to Fortune 500 companies. Her inspirational messages share valuable lessons about adapting to change, overcoming fear, and surviving in the face of tremendous odds. She challenges her audiences to remember, "the only limits we have are the ones that we create."

I am not a parent (yet), but I have been blessed with two incredible parents of my own, parents I have looked to at every stage of my career up to today. As a young athlete just beginning as a swimmer, my parents gave me the greatest gift I could have ever received: They taught me how to love the sport. That love has carried me through my career for 20 years and counting. Looking back on my athletic journey, I realize everything I have learned along the way has stemmed from that initial love—and it is because of that love that I had the courage to return to the sport following my paralysis at 18.

If I have learned one thing during my career, it is that you are only as good as the people with whom you surround yourself. It is because of my parents that I have gotten to where I am as an athlete and individual. As I have watched them deal with life's triumphs and tragedies, I have learned grace, compassion, and resiliency not only from their words but also their actions. My parents helped mold me into a **COMPLETE ATHLETE**, not by focusing on raising an athlete, but by raising me as a well-rounded individual. Because of that mindset, I have been able to establish a deep-rooted love and respect for my sport and recognize the vital role athletics has played in my life.

When I returned to the water in 2008, just two and a half months after my paralysis, I felt, in many ways, that I was returning as a Level 1 athlete. My parents are the ones who encouraged me, supported me, challenged me to dream big, and helped me commit to the sport that I had fallen in love with all over again.

It is my parents who taught me never to fall victim to circumstances, that we can always rise from disappointment if we choose to, and how to be resilient in the face of adversity.

Here I am, more than 20 years into my career, and if you asked me who my biggest role models are, I would still point to my parents. The impact my parents have had on my life from an early age has been a game-changer in terms of how I handle life's triumphs and tragedies. Those lessons have made me the person I am today. I know that, no matter the outcome of a competition, my parents are the two people who have always been and will always be there, and that has allowed me to dream fearlessly.

As you embark on this journey with your child, remember first and foremost that you are your child's parent. No matter how many medals hang on a wall or trophies sit on a shelf, your relationship is more valuable. Your children will always look to you, so lead by example. Teach them how to dream fearlessly, live with courage, act with compassion, and remember that being a **COMPLETE ATHLETE** extends far beyond their athletic pursuits.

To this day, my parents are still the first people I look for in the stands both right before and immediately following a race. They are a reminder of my past, representing the inner child in me and bringing a sense of calmness right before I swim. They symbolize the true meaning of "community."

No matter the outcome, they have picked me up when I have fallen, pushed me when I have been ready to give up, and been by my side in moments of disappointment and success. They are the bedrock of my community—my support team—representing everyone and everything that motivates me to swim.

Parents of athletes, you represent that same support for your child. Even though they may not know how to say it (or may be in a stage right now where they don't want to say it), you mean everything to them. As you encourage your child to become a whole person and a **COMPLETE ATHLETE**, remember you are an integral and irreplaceable part of that team.

Sincerely,
Mallory

Every night when my parents tucked my sisters and me into bed, my dad would say, "You're the best, you can make a difference, and you can change the world." It is amazing the impact such a simple phrase can have on one's life. Those words are the very words I have clung to in some of my greatest moments of adversity. I was paralyzed at age 18, yet two and a half months later, I was back in the pool. Over the course of the next four years, I set 15 World Records, 34 American Records, one Paralympic record and won both gold and bronze medals at the 2012 Paralympic Games. But this book isn't about the awards. Ultimately, it is about those 14 words my dad used to tell me every night.

I share these words with each of you reading this, knowing you are embarking on your journey toward becoming a **COMPLETE ATHLETE** at different times in your lives. Some of you may be in the early Level 1 stages of your career, and others are working through Level 3, dreaming of making it to Level 4 and potentially even Level 5. Regardless of where you are, you must understand the greater meaning of your athletic career. It is important to understand what it means to be a **COMPLETE ATHLETE**, what it takes to become one, and that however far you take this journey, someday when you look back, you will realize it was about far more than the athletic pursuit.

It is my hope you establish a deep-rooted love and respect for your sport, allow yourself to dream fearlessly, and learn the power of community. You will learn what it takes physically to be a great athlete, but never forget being a **COMPLETE ATHLETE** is about far more than your physical capabilities. Your sport will inevitably challenge you in ways you have never imagined. It will test your limits mentally, emotionally, and physically. But it will give you far more than you will ever be able to give back — and it will teach you how to live a life filled with passion, resiliency, and grit. Your sport will teach you how to be a leader, help you approach both success and failure with grace, and challenge you to adapt in the face of adversity.

As I look back at my own career, I have learned my greatest moments of glory as an athlete are about something so much greater than myself. While I have won a Paralympic Gold medal, one of my greatest victories came with a fifth-place finish. Something many may see as a failure has become one of the greatest moments of my career—all because of what it represented.

On September 17, 2016, I wheeled out onto the pool deck for my final race of the Rio 2016 Paralympic Games. As my name was announced, I saw nine people stand in the front row of the stands. For the past two years, I had been fighting back from a devastating injury that resulted in permanent nerve damage, robbing me of function in my left arm. Those nine people and so many others back home supported me day in and day out. We had days when the dream of Rio felt out of reach, but we never gave up.

As I approached lane 2 and looked to my loved ones and coach in the stands, I knew, regardless of what happened during the next few minutes, they would be with me every stroke. As I came in for the finish of my 200m Individual Medley, I looked to the scoreboard and saw a time that was a lifetime best and a "fifth place" next to my name.

I looked to the stands to those same nine people standing strong, cheering as loudly as they ever had. My future husband blew me a kiss. My parents and sisters were hugging each other and cheering. My coach stood tall in the middle with both arms in the air and tears in his eyes. In that moment, I realized there wasn't a medal in the world that could make that moment better than it already was.

As an athlete, some of our greatest moments of glory do not come with accolades; they come with so much more. They teach us that medals, records, and trophies do not define our careers; they teach us the power of our community and the will to never give up on our dream; they teach us to fall and pull ourselves back up; and they teach us the power of sport.

Throughout your career, you may fall, but it is my hope you rise again. Circumstances may step in and send you in a direction you never anticipated, but it is my hope you learn to believe you are superior to circumstances— and you have the power to choose how to react. You may get discouraged, but it is my hope, no matter how old you are, that you will fight for the inner Level 1 athlete in you who has just discovered an amazing joy and love for your sport. You will have doubters, but it is my hope that, rather than succumbing to the doubt, you allow it to fuel your flame. You will face failure, but it is my hope you will come to understand that to succeed you *must* fail because that is where you learn the most. Above all, it is my hope you will one day look back and realize your journey to becoming a **COMPLETE ATHLETE** was always about far more than your athletic pursuit—it is about the person you would become.

So, those words that my dad spoke to my sisters and me every night, that simple phrase—what does it stand for? What do those words mean? For me, they served as a reminder that no matter what the next day brought, I had parents in my life who loved me enough to tell me that I was the best, who believed in me enough to tell me that I could make a difference, and who hoped I would change the world. How does this relate to athletics?

Every day we choose to give our best, no matter how much or little we may have to give that day. And when we make that choice, we *will* make a difference and we *will* change the world. As you embark on your journey as an athlete, surround yourself with people who believe in you. Give your best every day. Give back to the sport that will give so much to you, and someday when you close the door on your athletic journey, do so knowing you left the sport better than you found it.

Now, in the meantime, go dream fearlessly and remember that as a **COMPLETE ATHLETE**, the glory doesn't come from a singular moment—it comes from the journey.

Sincerely,
Mallory

The role you play in shaping an individual, not only as an athlete but also as a person, is possibly more significant than you may even begin to realize. I have had some incredible coaches in my life, two of whom have left a lasting impact on both my career and my life. Because of these two men, I have learned there is a difference between truly loving the sport and simply loving to win— and the key to being successful as an athlete is becoming a **COMPLETE ATHLETE**.

In April of 2008, just two and a half months following my paralysis, I went to meet with a coach about the possibility of getting back in the water. That day was one of the most significant of my career. As I sat on the pool deck with my dad and we spoke to Jim, he treated me like any other athlete; he didn't look at me as someone with a physical impairment, but as a person and athlete. That day started our journey to the London 2012 Paralympic Games. In my five years of working with Jim, he taught me how to dream, how to set goals, and what it takes to reach them. He allowed me to realize my future could truly be limitless as an athlete if I was willing to work for it and focus on the fundamentals, as long as that love for the sport burned deep within me. Never once did he respond to my overly ambitious goals and tell me they were unrealistic. In fact, he encouraged those goals and often met them by upping the ante.

Jim and I went on to have an enormous amount of success in the sport. However, the greatest impact from my time with him didn't come from the awards we received, the records we broke, or the medals we won. The greatest impact came from the way he changed the course of my life by helping me grow into the athlete he challenged me to be. He came into my life at one of the most vulnerable times following my paralysis, and he became one of the first people in my life to see past my wheelchair and encourage me to dream bigger, set high-in-the-sky goals, and transition from hoping to believing.

Then there is Steve. He was one of my club coaches when I was a Level 1 athlete, and he coached both of my sisters and me throughout high school. Steve was crucial in helping me to establish my love for the sport as a young swimmer and a high school swimmer. It is because of that love that I was able to return to the water after my paralysis.

Going into London, I had had an incredible amount of success in the sport. However, in 2014, I suffered a very serious injury to my left arm, one that threatened to end my career. Not ready to retire, I turned to Steve to help me return to the sport. We had stayed in touch, but I had not swum under him since my senior year of high school in 2006. When I reached out to him after my injury, however, he believed in me at a time when no one else did—not even myself.

He helped me realize my love for the sport was purely that; it wasn't rooted in a love of winning but in a deep-rooted love and respect for swimming itself. In our two-year lead up to the Rio 2016 Games, my love for the sport grew deeper than ever because I went every day to the pool and found a coach at the end of my lane who believed in me, supported me, and pushed me to become stronger mentally, physically, and emotionally. Our journey to Rio had nothing to do with medals. Our journey to the Rio 2016 Games was all about redefining limitations, and I had a coach in my corner who allowed me to believe I was superior to circumstance, even when so many had given up on me as an athlete. As I look to continue my career going into Tokyo 2020, I will do so with Steve as my coach because I know he will continue to challenge me, and I know that we have so much left in our tank as a team.

I share these stories because both of these men have played a crucial part in my journey. As a coach, realize you will shape your athletes in ways that will transcend the sport. You will become a mentor, a role model, and (depending on the level you are coaching) potentially even a partner. As an athlete, you never get to a stage where you don't need your coach. For me, getting to the point where you trust your coach with all your being has made the greatest difference. When you get to a point in your relationship with your athletes where there is mutual trust and respect—and they know you have their back, no matter what—that is when you will be unstoppable together.

The success of any athlete's journey is not determined by medals or awards or records. Although I am far from being done as an athlete, I know someday I will hang up my suit and close the door on this chapter of my life. But the lessons I learned from my coaches will endure, so be sure to invest in your athletes not only as athletes but also as individuals. If your primary focus as a coach is the accolades of your athletes, you will always fall short as a team. However, if you focus on the journey and push your athletes to become **COMPLETE ATHLETES**, the potential is limitless.

Sincerely,
Mallory

Mallory

IN LEVEL 1

Athletes are embarking on their athletic endeavors in a manner that will likely set the tone for how they view the sport for the rest of their career. As these young athletes begin their journeys, it is important they do so with a strong foundation of love and respect for the sport and the greater athletic community.

It is never too early to begin thinking about how to become a **COMPLETE ATHLETE**. Even in the earliest years of playing a sport, a child can and should set personal development and technical growth as mutual goals. Practicing good character is every bit as important as practicing skills or endurance drills; in fact, it is even more important because a person's character lays the foundation for everything else that follows in life.

1.1 ATTITUDE

The first thing any athlete needs before beginning to practice or compete is a **POSITIVE ATTITUDE**—but positive about what? It's great to be optimistic about winning, but the ultimate outcome of a game, meet, or match has absolutely nothing to do with how you feel about going into a competition. You can have a positive attitude and still score fewer points or a negative attitude and still cross the finish line first. The earlier an athlete understands this important difference, the sooner he or she will appreciate one of the first and most important keys to becoming a **COMPLETE ATHLETE**.

ATHLETES » Consider two very talented athletes. Athlete A is someone who is often the fastest but is also arrogant, talks back to his parents or coaches, snaps at teammates, pouts after a loss, and is just generally down about everything. Athlete B is someone who may not always win but is fun to be around, speaks respectfully to adults, and encourages teammates. Athlete B may be disappointed by a loss, but uses it as motivation to work hard and perform better next time. Who would you rather spend time with? Who do you think coaches would rather have on their team? Who would you rather be?

I was not a standout swimmer in elementary school. I was good, but not great. Looking back, I can see how this actually became a huge advantage for me in later stages of my career. It gave me a chance to develop a love and respect for the sport, and I stayed with it because I wanted to, not because I felt I had to. My parents strongly emphasized the importance of having fun in competition instead of just winning. Their attitude allowed me to be a kid and have fun.

That didn't mean we weren't disappointed if we lost. It meant we stayed with it because we truly enjoyed what we were doing. This proved important later on as swimming became a way to find freedom and enjoyment rather than a place to feel pressure or obligation.

There were some kids who I competed with who swam because their parents bribed them, promising gifts if they made state or won their event. The result was often swimmers who would have a meltdown when they missed the cut or came in second place because they were competing for reasons other than sheer love for the sport, coaches, friends, community, and power of the water.

Years later, when I returned to the water after my paralysis, I found the freedom and happiness were still there because early on I had been given the opportunity to develop respect for my sport. I was able to find more joy in it than simply getting my hand to the wall ahead of someone else.

RESPECT

RESPECT means treating other people in a way that they feel valued, important, safe, and heard. In elementary grades, the most important aspect for athletes to work on is respect toward parents, coaches, officials, and other adults. Respect for your sport is also important. To become a **COMPLETE ATHLETE**, you need to understand the rules and regulations of competition and commit to following them.

ATHLETES >> Be sure to thank your parents for driving you to and from practice and competitions. Your athletic pursuits most likely require a huge time and monetary commitment from them. Make sure to show your appreciation. If you carpool with a teammate's parents, make sure to thank them for driving you as well.

When you arrive, be sure to greet your coach. You should also try to learn the names of your teammates so that you can address them by name. Players feel more respected when they believe they have an identity and other people care enough to get to know them.

PARENTS >> Remember many, if not most, coaches at this level are volunteers. Any support you can offer—whether coordinating a snack schedule, volunteering to help out in practice, or backing up the coach if other parents are being negative—will be greatly appreciated. Encourage your child to help clean up after practices or team meetings, and be prepared to pitch in yourself. This will help your child to not only develop a sense of responsibility but also recognize what respect for others looks like.

COACHES >> Make clear in the very first meeting how you would like to be addressed, whether by "Mr.," or "Mrs.," "Coach," or whatever name or title you prefer. By setting clear expectations right away, you help establish an environment of mutual respect.

Level 1 is all about learning, and it is important for coaches and parents to remember this. An important way to build respect is by conducting yourself in a way you want your child and teammates to emulate. Make sure to emphasize the positive aspects of the sports community as well. As young athletes begin to appreciate the hard work that goes into competing, in addition to the strong friendships that can result from teamwork, they will begin to develop a healthy respect for not only the people but also the sport itself.

Establishing respect early in the development of an athlete is crucial for long-term success both on and off the field of play. It will drive all other aspects of the athletic journey. Looking back on my own journey, the initial love and respect I developed as a Level 1 athlete gave me the tools to return to the water following my paralysis and constantly challenge myself to be my best version of a **COMPLETE ATHLETE**. Learning respect as a young athlete has a lasting impact, both personally and athletically.

Winning doesn't matter if you don't compete with integrity. It is essential young athletes learn the rules of their sport and commit to abiding by them.

ATHLETES >> Cheating is never okay. If you want to be a **COMPLETE ATHLETE**, you cannot have a "win at all costs" mentality. Instead, it is important to make sure you understand the rules and abide by them. This does not, however, mean you should be a tattletale. If you are concerned about something, talk to your parents or coach privately.

PARENTS >> Never badmouth your coaches in front of your child. If you disagree with a coach's style, speak with him or her privately or check with other parents to see if they share your concerns. Do not bash the coach in front of your child. Similarly, resist the urge to speak negatively about any other children on the team. Remember, youth sports are intended to be a learning experience, and everyone is there to develop and grow. Also, don't forget you are your child's most important influence, and he or she will imitate whatever you do.

*It is never too early to learn **SPORTSMANSHIP** toward friends and competitors. When children see friends from school on another team, you have a wonderful teaching opportunity to reinforce the idea they can be friends with competitors. This is also a good way to teach children the importance of learning to lose—and win—gracefully. Children should think about how they will talk to a friend at school the day after beating their friend's team. What if it were the other way around? How would they want their friend to talk to them?*

Athletes at Level 1 may also begin to consider the complexities of team dynamics. For example, if one teammate tripped on a ball or missed a catch at home plate but the team still won, that child gets to say he or she won. Some children may be bothered by this, while others have no problem with it. Many Level-1 athletes may struggle with a sense of "fairness." If parents and coaches take the lead in demonstrating good sportsmanship toward teammates as well as competitors, the athletes will follow.

1

2

3

4

5

TEAMWORK

Whether you are part of a true team sport, like soccer or basketball, or a more individualized sport, such as swimming or gymnastics, **TEAMWORK** matters.

An athlete's team is more than just peers on the field, in the pool, or on the court. Everyone who has a hand in making it possible for an athlete to participate in his or her sport is part of the bigger team.

PARENTS >> The ride home can be the best time to discuss teamwork. Remind your child that a loss is never just one person's fault, just as a win is not only one person's celebration. People are going to have good days and bad days, of course, but the process of winning or losing is much more than one race, game, or meet. It is the result of weeks of practice by the athletes, hours of preparation by the coach, emotional and time investment from people in the stands, and support for every player on the team.

COACHES >> Emphasize teamwork early and often. The more children feel connected to their peers on the team, the better they will learn to work together. Set aside a little time in each practice to work on learning each other's names. This important exercise helps them bond as a unit and feel good about their overall athletic experience.

It is essential that a **COMPLETE ATHLETE** *has a good sense of his or her team. Even if the sport is more individualized, like gymnastics or swimming, your teammates are the ones who train with you, push you to be better, and cheer for you. The key to having good* *teammates is being a good teammate. Be someone who encourages others instead of placing blame. This kind of attitude can set the mood and serve as an example for others.*

When I compete, it's only me in my lane. But I know that my teammates, coaches, husband, parents, sisters — the list goes on—are all cheering for me and pushing me to be my best. They are the ones who celebrate with me when I win and lift me up when I lose. The earlier athletes come to appreciate their team in the broader sense of the word, the more support they will have to draw from as they advance through the sport.

PROFESSIONALISM

Even though you are just starting in your sport, you can still show **PROFESSIONALISM**. Although you are not a professional in the sense that you are paid to participate in your sport, the way you present yourself and represent your team still matters and is part of becoming professional.

ATHLETES >> One important way to show professionalism is being ready when it is time for your parents to drive you to practice or for your carpool to pick you up. You should be changed into your practice clothes, shoes on, and any equipment you need in your bag. The same is true of game days, meets, or competitions. Rather than rushing around at the last minute looking for your uniform or hoping your socks are clean, have everything laid out the night before and be ready to leave your house on time.

PARENTS >> The way you behave at events not only sets an example for your child but also sets the tone for his or her entire athletic career. Showing enthusiasm and interest can inspire your child to keep trying; yelling at coaches or officials can embarrass your child or make him or her think it is acceptable to do the same. Be aware disinterest can also have negative implications. Of course, you may find it necessary to take a call or work on papers during practice. But if you are completely engrossed in your phone, book, or work that your child thinks you don't care about the event, he or she may not care either.

COACHES >> Take pride in what you do. Whether you are a full-time, part-time, or volunteer coach, you must convey to your players they matter to you and you take your investment in their development seriously. Be sure you show up to practice on time and dressed appropriately. Turn off your phone and stay engaged with your team during practice—and expect the same from your athletes.

At Level 1, professionalism is modeled by parents and coaches, so take this responsibility to heart. Parents can show professionalism by respecting practice and game times. Show up on time (or a little early for warmups) and pick up your child promptly afterward. I remember one coach telling our team parents are not setting their children up for success if they are not on time because the child misses out on valuable instruction time and does not learn responsibility and accountability for meeting obligations and working toward goals.

This idea of professionalism also extends to ownership of meeting responsibilities. A young child may not be capable of packing his or her practice bag alone, but if

the parent involves the child in the process, the child feels invested and develops a sense of responsibility. By the end of elementary school, a child should be able to be trusted to take some of these preliminary preparation steps alone. This sense of ownership is one of the most important steps on the path to professionalism for any **COMPLETE ATHLETE**.

LEADERSHIP

Just like anything else, **LEADERSHIP** is a skill that can grow and develop if purposely studied and practiced. At Level 1, most athletes are too young to take on leadership roles within their teams, but they can start learning what leadership involves.

PARENTS » Just as your child has responsibilities at home, he or she can begin taking on responsibilities pertaining to athletics. If your schedule allows, stay a few minutes after practice and encourage your child to help the coach clean up (or at least ask if there is a way to be of help). On the drive to and from practices and competitions, talk to your child about ways to show team spirit and a good attitude—no matter the outcome. This can help him or her learn how to rally the team and display positive behavior in any circumstance.

COACHES >> At this stage, the coach is the unquestioned leader of the team. When a child makes a catch or pauses before a play, he or she almost universally looks to the coach for a signal telling them what to do next. Stay engaged and encouraging.

Leadership skills come with maturity, but it is important to lay a good foundation early on. Kids at Level 1 are sponges; they absorb everything around them. The way a coach leads a team now will color a young athlete's understanding of leadership for the rest of his or her career. It is also important for parents to understand the way they lead their family has a direct impact on how children view leadership. Yes, you are your children's parents, and that makes you leaders in your family. Remember kids soak up everything. If athletics are a large part of your family's life and your children hear you trash-talking a team while watching a game, they will think this is appropriate behavior and take it to the field of play. Children look up to the adults in their life, whether older siblings, parents, coaches, or other role models. They emulate the behaviors and attitudes of these individuals.

1.2 PREPARATION

Thorough **PREPARATION** is the key to good performance. If you don't give your body the right nutrition and tools to help develop the right muscles and endurance, you will never be able to unlock all of your physical potential. This means eating balanced meals, limiting junk foods, and staying hydrated with water or natural fruit juices rather than sodas or other sugary drinks. A **COMPLETE ATHLETE** seeks to establish good habits now that will set the foundation for the rest of his or her life!

Parents and coaches should not be afraid to let their children learn about failure. The ability to deal with adversity is as much a skill as anything else in sports. Preparation is not solely about getting ready for a game or meet; it is about life itself. Learning to deal with disappointment is the first step in bouncing back.

Unfortunately, accidents are going to happen. A child may break his arm and be out for the rest of the season, or a child may face an injury that slows down her ambitions and goals for the year. Whatever the case, children need to have the mentality that allows them to focus on what really matters and appreciate the big picture. Remind your child and other players that missing a few games or even an entire season doesn't mean their career is over. It does mean they have been given the tools to learn how to prepare for disappointments and setbacks in athletics and in life. The more prepared they are to meet adversity head-on, the more resilient they will be.

1.3 FITNESS

In the first 10 to 15 years of your life, you will do more changing and growing than at any other time. While it is important to exercise to keep your growing body healthy, you must do so in a way that is safe for your bones, muscles, tendons, and ligaments. At Level 1, you probably don't need to focus on working specific muscles for your specific sport as much as you should focus on overall **FITNESS** and activity. Aim for 60 minutes of physical activity a day, whether from practice, playing outside, or taking your dog for a walk. Right now, the most important thing is learning to have fun in a variety of athletic activities you enjoy!

At Level 1, fitness is about learning to take care of your body and establishing love and respect for the sport. The healthiest decision you can make at this stage—for the short- and long-term—is just to enjoy being active. This should not be an age where children are worried about their physical appearance or weight, although, unfortunately, those struggles can begin as early as Level 1. Be sure to help your child and other athletes learn to simply enjoy being active. Whether taking the last part of practice one day and playing a game of tag or enjoying a fun family afternoon walk or bike ride, you should teach that a love for physical activity is the most important part of fitness.

As a young high school athlete, I always loved when our coaches would let us take the last part of practice and play a game of water polo or sharks and minnows. Some days, as spring and summer came around, our coaches would even pull us out of the water and let us enjoy an outdoor practice that had nothing to do with swimming. Instead, it allowed us to enjoy getting outside and being active as a team. To this day, we still play the occasional game of water polo at team camps to change it up and enjoy team building in a way that also keeps us physically active.

At every level, it is important to step back and make sure you are keeping the fitness component of the sport fun. After all, the more you love all aspects of the sport, the

more successful you will be as a **COMPLETE ATHLETE**. However, it is crucial that Level 1 athletes primarily focus on establishing a love for being active, whether with their team or family.

 ## TECHNIQUE

In any sport, there are basic skills, moves, strokes, or forms that are necessary to play the game or compete in races. This is the point of practice: to learn foundational skills so you can continue to build on them as you advance through different levels. This is why it is so important to be on time for practice and pay attention when your coach is talking. The **TECHNIQUES** will differ depending on the sport and rules of the game, which is what makes every sport unique and exciting!

COACHES >> It can be a real challenge to teach technique at this level. Some children will struggle with the most basic elements of physical coordination, while others simply have raw talent that makes them naturally able to take the correct stance or form. Both kids have an equal chance at success if they dedicate themselves to practice over the long term, but one will probably prove easier to coach than the other at this stage. The key is to take an individualized approach to meet each athlete at his or her level and to have copious amounts of patience as each child picks up the finer points of the sport at his or her own pace.

I've been to more than one swim meet where a parent gets angry at an official for disqualifying a child. The parent feels it is wrong to DQ an 8-year-old on a technicality and I can understand their point—but using proper technique is an essential part of learning to respect the sport. To understand proper form and rules of competition, young athletes need to learn what is and is not acceptable within the parameters of their sport, and parents should accept this as part of the growing process.

Coaches should strive to find a balance between teaching and enforcing fundamentals of the sport and keeping an emphasis on fun. Recently, I attended my 5-year-old niece's T-ball game. Even if a child got out, he or she still had a chance to run the bases to learn the different aspects of the sport. This seemed like a great compromise between teaching the rules and not allowing the competition to get too fierce at such an early age.

1

2

3

4

5

1.5 LIFESTYLE

Whether you are starting out or a seasoned pro, there will be more to your life than your sport. It is incredibly important you learn how to balance your academics, personal life, and athletics—especially as you advance further in your sport. You will have to consider a number of aspects on your journey to becoming a **COMPLETE ATHLETE**.

FAMILY

Your **FAMILY** should always be the most important people in your life. You parents and siblings are going to be the people by your side no matter where you go or what you do. Remember your family will love you no matter how well you compete. They love you on your good days as well as your bad days, and they care about how you feel and what you think.

ATHLETES ›#› Make sure your family knows you love them and appreciate the sacrifices they make to help you pursue your sport. Be respectful of their time and other responsibilities by doing whatever you can to help out, whether keeping your room clean, bringing your dirty practice clothes to the laundry room without being reminded, and helping out with the dishes after dinner or other chores around the house.

Remember your sport is not the only thing in your parents' lives; they have their own jobs and obligations. If you have brothers or sisters, they will have their own activities, hobbies, or sports that require your parents' attention, too. Be sure to be supportive of your siblings' activities, just as they are of yours.

The most important advice I can offer parents of Level 1 athletes is to be Mom and Dad—don't be Coach. Even if you are your child's coach, do not carry that role over at home. Let family time be family time. If you want to offer a few tips in the backyard or pool, that's OK, but don't let playtime turn into a full-on coaching session. This is true for every level, but it is most important in the elementary and middle school years when children are watching and copying everything you do—even if they aren't conscious of it.

Children are learning how to find balance in their lives. Encourage them to participate in a variety of extracurricular activities so they can explore all their interests and talents and learn more about themselves. There is absolutely no reason for a 10-year-old's schedule to consist of professional-level training or be limited to morning practice, school, homework, evening practice, and sleep. Often parents are so excited to see their children participate in the same activities they did when younger—or excel in a sport where they never did—that they begin to live vicariously through their child. Don't allow your passions or obsessions to limit your child's potential. I have always been grateful my parents allowed my sisters and me the leeway to find ourselves in our activities and test a number of different options to find the best fit for each of us. It kept us from burning out and, more importantly, allowed us to have a childhood. Kids need to be kids.

ACADEMICS

Even though **ACADEMIC** eligibility most likely will not become an issue until high school, it is still essential that Level 1 student-athletes learn to prioritize their schoolwork. Not every child is going to be an academic all-star, but every child can learn how to organize assignments, take responsibility for studying, prepare for quizzes and tests, and complete projects. Self-control in the classroom is also part of academics. Self-discipline behind the desk is a skill that translates directly to self-discipline on the field, on the court, or in the pool.

ATHLETES » Your schoolwork must always come before your sport. Whether you are in elementary school or college, your primary focus has to be your education. You should pay attention in class and ask questions about material you don't understand. Respect your teacher and your classmates, just as you would your coach and your teammates. Write down your homework and other assignments in a notebook so you don't forget about them. Make sure to tell your parents well in advance about upcoming tests or projects so you can begin working on them rather than scrambling around in a panic the night before they are due. If you set good study habits now, you will have a much easier time as your classes become more and more challenging in middle school and high school.

Level 1 is where everything starts. You have to find the balance now. If you wait until high school to start taking academics seriously, you are setting yourself up for failure. Parents, it is your responsibility to help your children find the proper balance between school, sports, and a social life.

SOCIAL LIFE

Young individuals must learn how to socialize with others their age. While sports can be a great way for this to happen, it should not be the only way. It is healthy for a child to make friends in school or within your homeschool group, at church, in civic groups or clubs, and with other children in the neighborhood.

PARENTS >> Encourage your child to spend time with different groups of peers in different settings so sports events are not the only place where socializing happens. If your child is naturally outgoing, talk about reaching out to new students or those who seem shy or reserved. If your child is naturally more withdrawn, try to find opportunities for play with just one or two other children so the situation does not feel intimidating or emotionally exhausting. While it is important for your child to be challenged, it is also important he or she

CHAPTER 1 » COMPLETE ATHLETE   45

not be forced into social settings that are drastically overwhelming.

COACHES » Rather than letting the kids form their own groups when pairing off for drills, you may find it more beneficial to assign partners, and to shuffle pairs at every practice. For children who are introverted, the prospect of having to pick a partner can be terrifying. Children who are extroverted, on the other hand, often relish the chance to work with a variety of teammates rather than their best friend every time.

At this age, sports can't be the only outlet; children need to have several different avenues for learning important skills and lessons through interaction with peers and adults. Some of my lifelong best friends are people who I swam with when I was younger, but that was because we developed relationships outside of the pool. I also have friends I made in choir, at church, and at school—in short, my parents encouraged me to bond with peers in ways that had nothing at all to do with sports. This, in turn, enabled me to learn social skills that weren't dependent on my practice schedule. It is vitally important children have different opportunities to develop relationships away from athletics. Sports friendships are inevitable, due to spending regular amounts of time together, but children need more to mature socially and emotionally.

Parents should keep in mind that, at this age, children are following the lead of the adults in their lives. If they see you obsessing over their sport or making it your only pursuit outside of family, they will likely follow that example and shut down any other opportunities.

ROLE MODEL

Every child should have at least one solid **ROLE MODEL** whom he or she admires, respects, and wants to imitate. Good role models serve as mentors by demonstrating responsible behavior, positive choices, and healthy ambitions.

PARENTS » At this level, parents are likely the most influential role models in their child's life, whether they or the child realizes it. Keep that in mind as you think about how you conduct yourself at practices, competitions, and everywhere else—public or private.

Talk to your child about role models. Whom do they admire? Why is that? What traits make a good role model? What traits make a poor one? By planting seeds early, you will help your child understand he or she has an active part in deciding what behaviors to emulate and which to avoid. This also helps lay the foundation for your child to see himself or herself as a role model when older.

When I was growing up, my biggest role models were the people right in front of me: my parents and my coaches. I'm sure if you'd asked me at the time, I would have insisted I was not imitating my parents. But now that I am grown, I can see how I really did look to them for their reaction in any given situation and how deeply that impacted my own emotional maturity. Although it is important children have numerous role models, it is also imperative for parents to be aware they are the greatest influences, especially at the earliest levels.

Since the influence is usually subconscious—and many children will resist associating their parents with being role models—surround your children with people who emulate the values you most want them to develop. Don't merely let them look up to popular people, but encourage them to look for role models who share your values. Children can hear about the importance of character all day long, but it will remain theoretical than real until they actually see it lived out. They will emulate role models who offer real-world, practical examples of ways to behave and compete.

Don't be afraid to nudge your child toward the right kinds of role models. If something happens and one of their heroes acts in a way that is less than heroic, use that as a jumping-off point for a dialogue about good versus bad decisions.

LIVING YOUR SPORT

The idea of **LIVING YOUR SPORT** means making it an important part of who you are and what you do.

ATHLETES >> Even though your sport should not be something you obsess over, it should be something you care about. Maybe you check out books from the library about your sport or choose an athlete you look up to for a school report. Maybe you find some time each week to practice on your own after school. To find real success in your sport as you advance through the levels, you must enjoy the pursuit and love what you do.

As you grow in your sport, don't be afraid to ask for help. Stay five minutes after practice to ask your coach about a specific drill or for help on a certain skill you need to master. As you begin to take ownership of your practice and dedication to studying your sport, the more your respect for the sport will grow.

Furthermore, as you develop true respect for your sport, you will find yourself wanting to learn more about it—its rules, history, most influential figures, more advanced techniques, most memorable moments. The more you educate yourself, the more your sport becomes a significant part of who you are.

JOIN THE CONVERSATION!

Live your sport & join the **COMPLETE ATHLETE** community of athletes, parents, and coaches by downloading the app today!

IN LEVEL 2

As athletes advance in their athletic journey, they will be challenged—physically, mentally, and emotionally—as they begin to come into their own, both as athletes and as individuals. It is important that Level 2 athletes extend to themselves the same respect they have built for the sport, and make healthy decisions to aid their changing bodies and more active lifestyles.

2.1 **ATTITUDE**

Level 2 can be a very intense time in a young athlete's life, with physical changes happening alongside a more intense academic course load, as well as increased demands from sports practice and competition. Emotionally, middle schoolers can feel confused and stressed as they try to figure out their place in the world.

The kind of **ATTITUDE** a student-athlete brings to these issues will affect everything else. A positive, enthusiastic outlook toward advancing in the sport while also maturing emotionally and socially will lay the groundwork for success, but that is easier said than done when social pressure and physical demands seem to complicate everything else.

The key issue for Level-2 athletes is figuring out how to begin investing themselves in the sport. Now that an athlete has a grasp on the fundamentals, how does he or she begin implementing them in a more meaningful way? Practice now requires a mental component, more than simply showing up for an hour a week and playing a game. More practice time may be required, and mental preparation is essential for putting aside a bad day to be fully present and engaged in practice or competition. Athletes are now mature enough to start thinking about being purposeful with their concentration and effort while participating in their sport.

RESPECT

RESPECT at this level is twofold. First, it is essential an athlete learn to respect his or her teammates.

Secondly, an athlete needs to begin developing a sense of respect for his or her own body.

ATHLETES >> Make sure your teammates feel valued and supported by you. While Level 1 placed emphasis on learning to respect the adults in your life, by Level 2, you should already be making a conscious effort to extend that same respect to your teammates. Whether you participate in a team sport or individual sport, the people you train with are part of your community and your support structure. It is essential you don't talk about them behind their backs, make fun of them, or make them feel discounted in any way. You are old enough to begin forming strong opinions on certain subjects; learning how to get along with someone who feels differently is a life skill. You may have one or two close friends on your team, but you need to show equal respect for everyone.

You must also learn to respect your body and all its capabilities. You may find you are suddenly much stronger than you used to be and your body seems to listen to you in ways it didn't previously. This can be incredibly exciting as you start to reap the benefits of paying attention to the fundamentals in Level 1. Middle school can also be frustrating sometimes—especially when your body seems to be growing in ways you don't like or changing in ways that make it harder to control it. Just when you think you have mastered solid technique, you may hit a growth spurt that seems to throw everything off, and you have to re-learn coordination and sometimes an entirely new form. These physical changes may present additional challenges along the way, but learn to embrace them as signs of your future powerful adult body.

PARENTS >> What you permit at home sets the stage for respect in every other arena of your child's life. Encourage your children to speak respectfully to and about their teammates at home. Badmouthing another player/teammate or not correcting your child when he or she does sends the wrong signal. The same goes for what you tolerate toward yourself; if your child is permitted to act disrespectfully toward you, he or she will believe that is an acceptable way to treat other adults, too.

With regard to your child's changing body, yours is one of the most influential voices in regard to how your child develops self-respect. Don't make your children self-conscious or tease them about the changes—or lack of changes—they are experiencing. Resist the urge to compare them to their friends or siblings; they are already self-conscious enough without feeling additional pressure from their parents over something they can't control. Instead, be patient and encouraging as they figure out how to move and manipulate their new muscles and changing shape.

COACHES >> Coaches also play an important role in how a Level 2 athlete learns respect for his or her own body. Remember, development affects each person in different ways and at different rates. Sometimes, an athlete may seem to become faster, more coordinated, and stronger overnight. Other times, an adolescent may actually seem to stop progressing or even go backward in ability.

This happens often during a growth spurt or other period of change as the body reroutes energy to other areas of the body and the child has to learn new ways to control strength. Patience and a willingness to re-evaluate individual approaches to training are essential in helping young athletes successfully navigate this period of transition with as little discouragement or frustration as possible.

The bodies of Level-2 athletes are beginning to change. These changes may happen rapidly, or they may happen slower than one would like. At this age, it is crucial to establish love and respect for your body.

I know a lot of athletes who struggled with the growth of their bodies, feeling self-conscious about their athletic build or self-conscious about their lack of strength. As athletes, we can be very hard on ourselves and on our bodies, but the earlier we learn to appreciate and respect our bodies, the better.

A boy may suddenly grow four inches over the summer, and everyone tells him he should be playing basketball. They think they are paying him a compliment, but he's really thinking, "How can I play basketball when I can hardly walk without tripping over my feet?" The opposite can be true too. A girl may think she has to give up her dream of playing volleyball because she is starting to carry weight differently from teammates and feels self-conscious in her uniform.

A boy may not start developing muscle mass as quickly as his teammates and get frustrated with his uncooperative body. It is important that these athletes don't disrespect their bodies, which can lead to body-image issues. If parents take the lead in encouraging their child to consider the positive side of these changes and coaches follow suit by adjusting their approach with each athlete, children can feel safe about growing and changing in a supportive and respectful environment.

My struggle with my body came much later in life. After my paralysis at 18, I had an incredibly difficult time learning to appreciate my new body. I felt self-conscious, insecure, and out of place in my own skin. I still remember the first time I went dress shopping following my injury; when I looked in the mirror in the fitting room that day, I just broke down in tears.

The reflection in the mirror didn't look like my vision of myself, and I didn't feel confident or comfortable in anything I tried on. I felt as though every image I saw was of individuals whom I no longer resembled. I began to resent my body and found it hard to love and easy to resent for what felt like limitations it imposed on me. All I could see were the four wheels attached to my backside and legs that got smaller and smaller with each passing day as muscle tone disappeared. It took quite some time for me to learn to appreciate my body and see my wheelchair as a tool to navigate this world rather than something that restricted me. That all started to change when I began swimming again. With each passing day in the pool, I began to respect my body for its ability to adapt. I soon realized my body served as the very vehicle that allowed me to chase my dreams.

SPORTSMANSHIP

Integrity is the backbone of **SPORTSMANSHIP**. A commitment to winning without gloating—and without cheating—and losing with grace is a hallmark of a **COMPLETE ATHLETE**. At Level 2, tryouts may become part of the picture. How does an athlete handle making or not making a team? What does this mean for the relationship between friends if one makes the cut and one doesn't? And how does sportsmanship translate to the outcome of competition?

The way an athlete learns to navigate those complicated dynamics is a major part of how he or she develops a sense of good sportsmanship.

ATHLETES >> It is important to show respect toward not only your teammates but also your competition. As your vocabulary grows, so might the urge to start trash talking your opponent; you may even find your teammates think you are really good at it. But are these really things a **COMPLETE ATHLETE** would say to or about the competition? There is a big difference between building up your own team and knocking down someone else.

PARENTS AND COACHES >> Don't shy away from having these conversations with your child or team. Explain to them, just as they are working to develop a personal respect for their sport, sportsmanship is carrying that respect outward to coaches, parents, officials, teammates, and—yes—even the competition.

A person can be a great teammate but a poor sportsman. Treating friends with respect doesn't mean you are demonstrating sportsmanship to the other people in your life. The attitude you carry—from practice to the huddle to the field of play—sets the tone for how other people will evaluate you and your entire team. Remember the attitude you bring to the field of play directly reflects not only yourself, but also your community.

TEAMWORK

At this level, team dynamics may be more complicated as scoring becomes more regular and wins versus losses affect team and individual rankings in a greater way than at Level 1.

In team sports, remember a loss is not one person's fault nor is a win one person's victory. However, in individual sports, two teammates may be in direct competition in individual events; suddenly, there is a dual relationship of teammate and competitor.

ATHLETES >> Encouraging your teammates can be one of the best ways to foster **TEAMWORK**. If your teammates know you have their back, they will have yours, too. Be the kind of friend you want to have.

Nonetheless, when you take the starting block, you may be going head-to-head against someone with whom you have become friends with at practice. This can be a very complex dynamic. How do you relate to someone who is both your friend and rival? It may help to keep in mind that you are making one another better; as you train together day in and day out, you are pushing each other to stretch your skills and improve as athletes. Your teammates are part of your community, and you are part of theirs. Your community is there to support you and help you grow, and you and your teammates are doing that for one another. Just as they make you better by challenging you, you are helping them, too. As the old expression goes, "A rising tide raises all boats." In other words, as one person on a team improves, everyone else on the team will also as they all develop better skills, techniques, strength, and speed to keep up.

As you mature in your sport, remain humble. Your teammates are instrumental in helping you stay this way. They will be your biggest supporters, but they will also be quick not to let your success go to your head. The better you do as an individual, the more you can be sure your teammates are working even harder to ensure they keep up with you—or even surpass you!

PROFESSIONALISM

Level 1 places an emphasis on developing respect and love for the sport. Level 2 athletes are now carrying this out by having pride in what they do, how they present themselves, and taking care of their equipment and field of play.

ATHLETES » As you become more serious about your sport, you should take increasing pride and ownership in what you do. Instead of merely showing up for practice and being done for the week, you should begin looking for opportunities to practice on your own outside of scheduled practice hours. You should begin to set reasonable and achievable training goals, doing more than just the minimum.

Now that you are old enough to understand the fundamentals of your sport, you are mature enough to appreciate and respect the infrastructure of the entire sport. This means you treat your equipment and the team's equipment and training facilities with pride. Help clean up after practice and store equipment in a neat and organized way that helps keep it in good working order.

You should also take pride in yourself. Shower regularly, keep your hair, clothes, and equipment clean, and use necessary sanitary items such as deodorant.

PARENTS >> As your child is becoming increasingly independent, it is important he or she takes on more responsibilities. Your child should be capable of washing practice clothes every day and making sure the required uniforms are clean, packed, and ready for competition. However, just because your child may show signs of maturity and independence (or probably likes to remind you of that fact), he or she still needs parental guidance and the occasional reminder to keep those proverbial ducks in a row. It may be necessary to remind your child to do laundry or take a shower every day. One of the biggest challenges of parenting at Level 2 is finding that balance between holding your child accountable and letting him or her learn while still providing the support and instruction that is an essential part of developing personal responsibility and maturity.

COACHES >> Encourage your players to take ownership of their sport by assisting with setting up and taking down equipment for practices. This may sometimes take a little bit longer than it would if you did the job by yourself. However, you are developing **COMPLETE ATHLETES**, and teaching your athletes to take responsibility for and pride in their facilities is just as important as time spent training.

As you grow as an athlete, it is vital you do so with a level of professionalism. Although you may think it is too early in your career to worry about that component, the fundamentals start now in demonstrating respect for your community, the equipment you use, and the field of play. At Level 2, we talk a lot about the value of respect because it plays into every component of your development as a **COMPLETE ATHLETE**. *Your ability to respect teammates, coaches, parents, officials, and the community as a whole plays into professionalism. Soon you will be a Level 3 athlete, potentially working toward Level 4. As you grow as an athlete and a person, the way you handle yourself professionally is a reflection of both you and the community you represent. Be mindful of all the components of your sport and take pride in the sport you have grown to love.*

LEADERSHIP

At this level, **LEADERSHIP** will probably come in the form of one team member setting an example by showing inclusion rather than exclusion.

Sports can get cliquey, both in terms of how team members act toward outsiders as well as form cliques within the team. Cliques of any kind should be discouraged and within a team environment, they can be toxic. Many adults tend to think of cliques as a problem with adolescent girls, but in reality, they can crop up anywhere and be extremely damaging to the team as well as to the individuals excluded. Young athletes who are determined to see beyond the pettiness of these divisions and who are willing to reach out to others are the ones who will naturally begin to emerge as team leaders due to their character.

ATHLETES » The "Golden Rule" is a great starting point for anyone who wants to develop as a leader: Treat others the way you would like to be treated. Some people try to gain power by drawing lines and determining who is "in" and who is "out," but you have far more influence if you lead by example and truly earn the respect of all your teammates.

PARENTS » Discourage your child from participating in any kind of behavior that intentionally excludes another teammate. It is natural, of course, for a child to be closer to a certain friend on the team, but that doesn't mean the player has to talk to, partner with, or even pass to that friend exclusively. Look for organic opportunities to bring in other teammates. Adolescents can easily detect when gestures are artificial or patronizing, but something as simple as inviting another teammate to join the carpool can help break down any walls that might be starting to form.

COACHES ≫ When you spot athletes exhibiting good leadership, be sure to reward them. This doesn't mean you necessarily call attention to what the athlete is doing (though it might). However, extending a special privilege, such as leading warmups, to someone who is being a good role model can help reinforce the idea that real leadership comes from character, not just talent.

PREPARATION

By Level 2, an athlete is mature enough to take a deliberate approach to preparing mentally for training and competition. As an adolescent becomes more serious about training for his or her sport, proper **PREPARATION** becomes increasingly important. It's no longer enough to simply show up for an hour a week and expect that to be enough; now a higher level of personal investment and full preparation from all standpoints is required.

ATHLETES ≫ If you don't put forethought into practice and just go through the motions when you get there, you are cheating your teammates as well as yourself out of your best effort. You are now at an age where you should be setting realistic training goals for yourself and then consciously working to achieving them in every practice, game, or meet—and this includes being mindful of what you put in your body. Take a few moments each day to mentally prepare yourself for what you want to accomplish and how you plan to do so through physical fitness, skills training, and good dietary choices. Setting aside even a few minutes to ensure you are making good decisions and setting reasonable goals can go a long way toward getting your head in the right place to make the most of your training or playing time.

PARENTS ›› As the parent, you are the one who is ultimately in charge of your child's diet. While you may not be able to control what they eat when they are at school, you can keep healthy options on hand for snacks, pack healthy lunches, and offer breakfast and dinner options that are well-balanced and appetizing. By helping your child fuel his or her body in the right way, you are helping to grow a **COMPLETE ATHLETE** who can evaluate food choices and make wise decisions.

There is a big difference between showing up to practice and going through the motions and showing up to practice and being mindful of your training. This is something that starts at Level 2 and will carry all the way through Level 5. Your ability to be mentally, emotionally, and physically prepared for training and competition will make the difference in your athletic career. The same goes for your personal life and academics. When you spend time with family and loved ones, it is important to be present and engaged, instead of just being there physically but not mentally or emotionally. In your training, simply running through drills without focusing on them will not help you grow or improve as an athlete. You must realize that everything you do outside of training directly impacts your ability to train at full capacity.

As I trained for the Rio 2016 Games, I was coming off a very serious injury. I knew that, more than ever in my career, I had to focus on the simplest components of my swimming if I wanted to improve. Even as a Level-5 athlete, it is easy to show up to practice when you are

tired and worn down from the week and just go through the motions to finish up, but you have to challenge yourself to constantly be mentally present. The mental preparation for me became just as important, if not more important, as I went into the 2016 Paralympic Games. This is a skill set that is crucial in all stages in your athletic career as well as your life.

 FITNESS

While Level 1 emphasized athletes laying the groundwork for an active lifestyle, the emphasis at Level 2 needs to be learning to listen to their bodies and responding appropriately. Because of the many changes a child's body undergoes during this time, he or she may suddenly find difficulty with skills that were once easy or not know when pain is a sign of growth versus a sign of injury.

PARENTS >> Your child may begin to obsess over mastering a certain skill or fitness goal to a degree that you find worrisome. There is a fine line between admirable dedication and unhealthy obsession that can lead to an overuse injury or other problems. Encourage your child to actively pursue his or her goals, but also keep close tabs on just how much time is spent repeating the same activity. Most parents usually tell by intuition alone if their child is dedicated to adapting his or her training to meet the new demands of a changing body or if a child is asking things of still-developing joints and muscles that just aren't possible, reasonable, or safe.

COACHES >> Coaches are especially important in providing personalized tweaks to the training schedule for young athletes going through a particularly difficult growth period. A child may not be well-enough attuned to his or her body at this point to make the distinction between good pain and bad pain.

Does being out of breath signal a child needs to work on endurance, or is it a sign of an impending asthma attack? When does a sore muscle mean it has been broken down in a good way so it can rebuild stronger, and when does it indicate there is an actual injury?

While a coach cannot make a definitive diagnosis unless he or she is actually trained in the medical field, it is a coach's responsibility to be educated on the basics of youth sports injuries so that he or she can make an educated guess about what a child's body is undergoing and make adjustments to training accordingly.

2.4 TECHNIQUE

At Level I, the emphasis should be on learning the fundamentals of the sport while having fun in practice and competition as part of an active lifestyle. At Level 2, athletes should be focusing on implementing those fundamentals as they grow their skills and ability.

ATHLETES >> To become better, prioritize the development of your technique and form over striving to become the biggest, fastest, or strongest. Constantly reassess your technique and make any adjustments necessary as your body grows and changes. Good technique helps protect you from injuries and become a better all-around athlete.

This can be a real challenge if sloppy form results in a better time or a faster pitch than proper technique. Remember you are establishing habits now that will train your body to react in competition. If bad technique is part of your muscle memory, your performance is going to suffer in the long-run.

COACHES >> It can be really tough to stay committed to fundamentals when parents are demanding results to make sure their hard-earned money is paying for training that actually benefits their child's performance. In a lot of cases, cutting corners with form can make an athlete's statistics appear higher or make it seem as if a younger child has mastered a more advanced move. Remember, though, your first responsibility has to be to the overall health and safety of your athletes, and that means setting them up for success later by protecting their bodies and educating them about the proper way to execute a maneuver or skill.

As you continue to invest more time and energy in your development as an athlete, don't forget to slow down from time to time to reassess where you are. It may seem counterintuitive at times, as taking the time to tweak your skills or completely change your technique can often inhibit your performance for the short-term. However, do not sacrifice long-term gains for short-term gains. In all respective sports, technique is crucial for further development as you continue to get stronger. Now is not the time to establish bad habits, even if they may seem easier for you to do.

I cringe when I am watching high-level youth sports competitions and see athletes repeatedly using poor form purely because they do not want to invest the time and have the patience to fix it. You will notice this in sports across the board—running and swimming, gymnastics and cheerleading, baseball and soccer. In all of them, you need to step back and focus on the fundamentals as your body is growing and becoming stronger. For many, this process can be frustrating, and it is easier at times to fall back on bad habits rather than stick it out and be patient. You typically notice athletes giving up on their focus of changing form and tweaking technique when they are frustrated with the time it takes to see improvement. When frustration sets in, athletes need to remind themselves establishing correct technique and form will help them develop in the long run. Disregarding proper technique can be problematic because it can lead to injury, from a stress fracture or overuse injury to more serious injuries as you age.

Level 2 is the perfect time for athletes to begin perfecting form. Now that they understand the fundamentals, they can start to train their bodies to make the proper position second nature. Remember, what you practice in training becomes muscle memory come competition, so if you are sloppy with your technique in training, you can't expect it to all come together during competition or on game day. Practice makes perfect, so challenge yourself in training. Move down to a slower lane for a little while to perfect your stroke even if you feel as though you are sacrificing speed and performance for a technicality. That investment in your athletic career and your health will absolutely be worth it in the long run.

JOIN THE CONVERSATION!
Get the latest advice from your coach and the pros in the **COMPLETE ATHLETE** app!

Personal responsibility should be increasing as children become adolescents. Young athletes are transitioning from elementary school toward the much higher stakes of high school competition. The middle school years are a kind of bridge between those two periods and a very important time to master life skills such as time management and prioritizing commitments. At this age, it's all about finding balance.

It might sound a little funny, but this period is one of trial and error as young people learn how to navigate the challenges of being a serious student-athlete without the stakes being quite as high as they will be in high school. This is also a great time for parents to back off a little bIt and let their children explore their independence— but still be right at hand when they are needed. Middle schoolers love to think of themselves as tremendously mature, but they still need their parents more than most are willing to admit. In this way, too, Level 2 is about finding balance.

FAMILY

Middle school is a time when friendships may be fickle, but **FAMILY** is forever. It is important both kids and parents remember this.

ATHLETES » You are getting to an age where you have started to form your own opinions about all sorts of things, from what sports teams or players you like to various social issues. It can be tempting to think you know everything there is to know about a subject. While you may be very well-read on a subject or believe in an issue very strongly, you should always keep in mind you are still growing and your parents might understand more about something than you think. Your parents may frustrate you when they hold you accountable for your actions or challenge your choices, but they are just doing their job, which is to be your parents. Even though you are becoming more independent, you still need your parents and your siblings. Friends may come and go, hurt your feelings sometimes, or make you feel left out. But your family members will always be your biggest fans and greatest support system, so don't be so quick to dismiss them.

PARENTS >> Structure your home life in a way that encourages success through effective time management. Be sure you model how to live your priorities. Keep a **FAMILY** calendar in a prominent place so that everyone can see when each member of the family has commitments. This helps forge a respect for everyone's time and individual pursuits and responsibilities.

Middle school is a time when your kids need you. Even though they may sometimes be difficult and even try to push you away, they still desperately need your guidance and love through this challenging age. Celebrate their victories and make sure they feel supported and loved unconditionally, even on days when they forgot their homework or play poorly.

ACADEMICS

One of the biggest transitions from elementary school to middle school is going from being in one classroom with one teacher for every subject to changing classes for the first time. This requires a whole new level of organization to keep track of which folders correspond to which class and to keep projects and different homework straight. Students are also getting more choices in their curriculum. Electives such as music, art, and languages are added.

Students may feel overwhelmed by the sudden plethora of choices before them: Choir, orchestra, or band? (And if orchestra or band, which instrument?) Drama, visual arts, or dance? Spanish, French, German, Latin, Chinese, or Sign Language?

While students need to learn to take responsibility for these new pressures, parents and coaches need to be present to provide guidance, support, and assistance as middle schoolers feel their way through this new phase.

ATHLETES » Time management is a life skill you will need to have figured out *before* you get to high school, and middle school is your best opportunity to do so.

Keep in mind teachers don't always coordinate workloads with one another, so you may find you have a heavy homework load of pre-algebra, history, and science all on the same night. How do you manage to get it all done? What if that heavy homework night also happens to be the evening of a practice or game?

The stronger your time management skills, the more likely you are to navigate these challenges successfully. If you are well-organized, writing your assignments down and knowing when they are due, there will be no scrambling to find your books (or potentially forgetting them at school) and no wasting time trying to remember which pages you've been assigned. You will be able to lay out a clear schedule for what homework you will do on the bus on the way home, what you will complete before practice, and if necessary, what you will complete after practice.

This is even more true when it comes to completing projects. If you are organized and keep track of your assignments in a planner or on a calendar, you can keep track of when projects and papers are due and can work on them a little bit each night so you are not having to cram in a week's worth of work the night before—and possibly at the same time you are supposed to be at practice or competition.

PARENTS >> You must let your children learn the cost of poor time management by allowing them to face the consequences sometimes, but that doesn't mean they need to be left to fend entirely for themselves. Perhaps it would be helpful to review your child's homework planner every evening and discuss any upcoming projects once a week. You should also remind your child to buckle down and get to work if he or she is distracted or procrastinating. However, this does not mean you should stay up late to finish your child's project that he or she forgot about until the last minute or you need to leave work to run his or her backpack to school if they forgot it when they overslept in the morning. Supporting your child means doing everything you can to set them up for success in the long run—and this means helping them learn to take ownership of their assignments as well as teaching them the repercussions of their actions and choices.

COACHES >> Remember your players are students before they are athletes. That means that, should parents choose to bench their child until grades improve, you need to be supportive. It also means, while your athletes have a responsibility to work hard for your team, their academics are a higher priority. Be sensitive to the rhythm of the school year and consider scheduling shorter practices the week of standardized tests or other major events. These kids are still middle schoolers, after all, and they are still learning how to prioritize their commitments.

JOIN THE CONVERSATION!
Follow and chat with your coach and team-mates in the **COMPLETE ATHLETE** app!

SOCIAL LIFE

Middle school social life is usually difficult whether or not sports are involved, but it can become even more complicated—in both good and bad ways—with that extra element.

As multiple schools combine into one middle school, finding new friends can be intimidating. The same is true a few years later when several middle schools may combine into one high school. Having an instant group of friends from an athletic team can greatly ease this transition. However, as mentioned before, this is also an age when cliques start to form and often become an issue. Therefore, athletes, parents, and coaches must work together to help adolescents develop a healthy and age-appropriate social life, honing and shaping those social skills that will be valuable at every age.

ATHLETES >> Because you are starting to spend more time in practice and travel to and from competition, it is natural for your teammates to become close friends. This goes a long way toward developing a sense of team spirit and teamwork. As in Level 1, however, you need to get to know your teammates outside of the sports setting; learn to relate to them in ways beyond your interactions when passing a soccer ball or shooting layups. Learn how to interact with people and form friendships in a variety of situations, from school to sports to civic groups to neighborhood kids to church friends. Making friends is not a skill that comes naturally to everyone, and it is one that requires practice for even the most outgoing person, so it will be a huge bonus for you to practice it often.

At Level 2, you also must learn how to be inclusive. If you and a few of your teammates are planning to go out for burgers after a game, why not invite the whole team? What will you gaining by limiting that outing to a few select people? Sometimes, of course, there will be times when you want to do something with your very closest friends from the team—maybe your parents said you could take one friend to the movie or invite your two best friends over for a sleepover.

If that is the case, don't talk about those plans at practice in a way that will make your other teammates feel left out. How would you feel if some of your friends talked loudly about a party they were having, but you were not invited? How do you think others feel when you do the same thing? And, of course, remember to make friends outside of your team as well. Just because someone doesn't share your love for a certain sport doesn't mean you won't have other things in common.

PARENTS >> Teamwork will naturally meld over into social life, and this is a good thing. Be careful, however, of falling into the same adolescent politics you want your child to avoid. It always feels good to see your child thriving socially, but intentionally guide your child toward becoming someone who invites rather than shuns. Your family will probably enjoy spending more time with certain families on the team; that's just the way different personalities meld or clash.

But don't let your own preferences spill over into your child's team dynamics. If you want to get together with another family or two over the weekend, don't broadcast it or turn it into an unofficial team meeting with only a select few in attendance. If any decisions or team policies are made, make them in a setting where everyone is invited. You, as the parent, should take the lead with including people. Set the example for your child.

COACHES » A great way to combat cliques is to plan team-building exercises outside of competition or practice. By moving your team to a different setting and coming up with creative ways to mix up groups and force your athletes to interact with different teammates, you can help them form new bonds and build trust with those outside their main group. Every coach knows that good team chemistry is worth its weight in gold; purposeful team-building events—even once or twice in a season— go a long way toward developing that chemistry.

As do parents, you set the example and the expectation of what is acceptable. The members of your team are naturally going to have one or two closer friendships, but leaving people out and intentionally excluding or shunning someone does not foster team.

I've seen teams where a small group of athletes got together to make spirit signs to hang around the training facility in an effort to promote team spirit. The problem? They didn't invite the rest of the team beyond their own little circle. The result was a lot of hurt feelings rather than team encouragement. I've also seen parents who seem to feed on their child's popularity and relish the role of being one of the "in" families—a role they can only maintain by keeping other people "out."

The rule of thumb should always be if the outcome of the gathering will affect the team, everyone should be invited. Of course, there are going to be people who can't make an event or aren't interested, but the invitation should be extended. If an athlete wants to practice jumps or passing one-on-one with another teammate, that is one thing. However, if a handful of people plan a thank you for the coach, decide to get special shirts printed, or want to revise the snack schedule but don't ask everyone to be involved, then you have a problem. Inclusion benefits everyone. It's just common sense. A united team will perform better and allow everyone a more positive overall experience.

ROLE MODEL

When children are younger, they tend to mirror whatever their parents do. If the parents cheer for a certain team or a particular athlete, the child usually does too. By Level 2, however, young people have often started deciding for themselves who their favorites are —and they may not be the same as mom's or dad's.

PARENTS >> Adolescents feel empowered when they make their own decisions. At this age, the people they choose to be their **ROLE MODELS** will have an influence on how they develop. Get involved. Ask your child not just *whom* they admire but *why*. Don't be afraid to challenge your child to answer this question: What is it about this individual that makes him or her worthy of your admiration? Level 2 athletes will often mimic their role models with their reaction to scoring a goal or crossing the finish line. Ask your children if they want other people to associate them with the person they are imitating.

You know best the standards and behaviors you want your child to emulate. Educate yourself on anyone your child picks as a hero, and make sure that person shares your values. The role model your child looks up to will ultimately shape the role model he or she becomes.

Kids this age want to feel empowered, take ownership, become independent, and often skip ahead to the teenage years. But they are still young and impressionable. Solid parental guidance is key to helping them think critically about characteristics of good role models. This, in turn, will lay the groundwork for developing into role models themselves as they advance in their athletic career.

A person is the culmination of all his or her decisions, and this is especially true for athletes. Even at this young age, the choices a person makes during the day will affect his or her performance on the field, on the court, in the pool, or on the mats. There is a fine line between taking ownership of one's goals and being obsessed with them, but Level 2 athletes are mature enough to begin considering how all the little decisions add up to positive or negative outcomes.

ATHLETES >> One of the most important ways you can **LIVE YOUR SPORT** is by remembering you are an athlete even when you are not in practice or competition. This means the food you eat, what you drink, and even the amount of sleep you get all contribute to how you will perform in the classroom and in your sport.

Before you are tempted to stay up late to watch TV, ask yourself if the extra 30 minutes or hour would be better spent practicing a skill, reading about strategies or heroes of your sport, or even getting extra rest. What if you procrastinate on a project and have to stay up late to get it finished—but have a game the following night? Was it worth losing sleep ahead of a big day in order to goof off during the week?

Everything has a compound effect. Look for opportunities to work outside your sport to improve and think about how your actions outside of practice affect your performance. Living your sport means you must make your educational responsibilities your priority, commit to healthy decisions, practice deliberate mental preparation, take pride in everything you do, and allow yourself to gain all the tools you need to succeed in working toward your goals. All of these together are what make a **COMPLETE ATHLETE**.

As you begin to integrate living your sport into everyday life and realize the implications your decisions outside of training and competition have on your performance, it is also important to maintain a healthy balance on this. Regardless of if you are a Level 2 athlete or a Level 5 athlete, hyper-focusing can be detrimental to your career. Be sure that, as you begin to challenge yourself to live your sport in all aspects in your life, you do so with a healthy balance.

Focusing on the physical impact sleep, nutrition, and recovery have on your overall performance is beginning becoming important, but also embrace to fun part of living your sport! If you have the opportunity to choose a topic for a school project, consider doing something in relation to your sport or a role model, allowing yourself to integrate your passion for sport into your academics. As you begin to integrate your lifestyle and your sport together, be sure you do so with balance for the other priorities in your life.

IN LEVEL 3

As athletes start to feel the pressure of their own goals and aspirations and look toward college, it is important they continue to make smart and healthy decisions that will continue to push them both on and off the field of play. It is important in Level 3 that athletes take time to focus on their commitments in every aspect of their life.

③.¹ ATTITUDE

ATTITUDE is a word thrown around quite a bit when it comes to teenagers—sometimes with a very negative connotation. Whether this is fair or not, the fact is attitude is a major factor in the performance— and ultimately, the degree of success—of a **COMPLETE ATHLETE**. Your attitude colors every aspect of your practice, mindset, relationships, and even reputation, so it is important to run a regular "attitude audit" on yourself to make sure you are not allowing outside influences to affect you in undesirable ways.

RESPECT

At Levels 1 and 2, the emphasis on **RESPECT** is learning how to show it toward other people. By the time an athlete reaches high school, he or she must learn how to show respect inwardly as well as outwardly. These years can be such a challenging mix of new freedoms, experiences, temptations, and pressures. The best way to steer teenagers toward making good choices is educating them on the importance of self-respect and respect for their values.

ATHLETES » By Level 3, you should have already learned to have a healthy respect for your coaches, your teammates, and the amazing capabilities and potential of your own body. All of these continue to be important in Level 3. This means even though you may have a different opinion on a game strategy or practice technique, you defer to your coach. You can express your ideas in a calm and non-accusatory tone, but ultimately, you need to accept your coach's leadership as the final word for the team. You should also show respect and appreciation to your parents for their support and encouragement as you continue progressing in your athletic career. They have been your biggest and most consistent fans this whole time, so don't take them for granted or belittle them. You owe them so much more than that.

You also need to show respect for your teammates. Encourage them in practice; congratulate them on their successes; don't blame them if they had a bad play or disappointing leg in a relay. Make sure your teammates feel safe with you and trust you will not gossip behind their backs or make them feel unvalued in any way.

As a Level 3 athlete, you also need to make sure you respect yourself and your capabilities. This self-respect extends even further now as you learn to respect what you stand for. Don't beat yourself up over mistakes and don't allow others to put you down. Respect your health and your future by refraining from drugs, alcohol, or any other behaviors that could damage your body or have long-term consequences. With so much peer pressure and social stress, you may feel pulled in several directions on any number of issues. A crucial part of showing respect is respecting yourself and your values by staying true to what you believe.

PARENTS >> Respect begins at home. The way a teenager is allowed to speak and act toward his or her family members sets the bar for all other interpersonal interactions. One thing college coaches consistently look for in a potential recruit is the way the athlete acts toward his or her parents. This conduct is incredibly revealing about the student's overall attitude, teachability, and ability to work well with others.

Obviously, you should want your child to be respectful and positive simply because that is how well-adjusted individuals act, but the added element of the recruiting process makes this an even more important behavior to emphasize in your home.

Respecting values extends to you, too. Don't be afraid to hold your teenagers responsible for the decisions they are making. As they reach the teenage years, they are naturally going to become more independent and start forming their own beliefs, but as a parent, you know better than anyone else the core values and standards you want them to maintain as they go through life. For example, if faith is something your family holds as important, don't be afraid to push back if your teens suddenly no longer want to attend church.

Explain that it has always been part of their life, and they aren't going to suddenly stop going just because they think it is no longer cool. It's your job to keep your children on track and remind them of the core principles with which they have been raised.

COACHES >> Unfortunately, it can be easy for a star athlete on any team to become a little bit too full of his or her talent and overall contribution to the team's success. If you see this pattern beginning to emerge in certain players, it may be necessary to have a team meeting or even a one-on-one conversation to discuss what respect means in all its forms, why it matters, and the difference between self-confidence and arrogance.

Make sure to have candid discussions with your athletes about respecting team values as well. Remind them to make clean decisions both on and off the field of play and to make choices that lead them toward becoming both better athletes and people.

My high school coach, Steve, had such a significant influence on my life during my teenage years. He was someone who was not afraid to kick my tail if I needed it, but he also knew when life came before sports. He took things seriously, but not so much that he ever lost sight of the people he was coaching. Coaches are some of the most important mentors in the lives of young people, and I was fortunate enough to have a coach who modeled his values of integrity, hard work, and making family a priority. Watching the way Steve incorporated a respect for his values into his professional life inspired me as an individual and impacted me greatly. In fact, I respected his way of living and working so much that he became my primary coach years later as I trained for the Rio 2016 Paralympic Games and is still my coach as I work toward the 2020 Tokyo Games!

As introduced in Level 2, **SPORTSMANSHIP** toward the competition continues to be important. For athletes hoping to compete on their high school teams, they will first have to face tryouts and the challenge of making varsity or junior varsity. Additionally, teammates from club sports may now become rivals during the high school season if they live in neighboring districts. A teen working to become a **COMPLETE ATHLETE** needs to be able to navigate these situations with sportsmanship and maturity.

Sportsmanship among one's teammates matters as well. It is easy to show good sportsmanship when your team is doing well and everything seems to be going your way; it's a lot harder when a member of your team makes a major mistake or has a setback that contributes to a loss or a lower ranking for all of you. At Level 3, the stakes are higher than they have ever been, and tempers can sometimes flare when someone makes a blunder in major competition. While it is obviously important to learn how to keep emotions in check and to support a teammate when he or she is responsible for the error, it can be more difficult for a young athlete to learn how to show good sportsmanship to himself or herself in a similar situation.

ATHLETES >> Some athletes will be thrilled to make any team representing their school, while others might have their heart set only on varsity. Your attitude about the team you make says a great deal about who you are as a sportsman. If you make varsity as an underclassman, don't be tempted to become arrogant; you still have a lot to learn. If you don't make varsity, don't think that means you should give up on your dream entirely and don't sulk throughout the season. Instead, focus on the opportunities to not only develop your skills further but also be a leader on your team for younger players.

Don't neglect to extend sportsmanship to yourself. Mistakes are going to happen; it's just part of life. Sometimes, the mistakes are relatively minor, like stepping on the line in your floor routine for a small point deduction or not making solid contact with the ball when you hit it. Sometimes the mistakes are bigger, like a false start that disqualifies the entire relay team or a missed pass that results in a turnover. Whatever the case, your reaction needs to be twofold: You need to own your part in the error, and then you need to move on.

Owning your mistake means you don't make excuses or argue with officials. If you genuinely believe their call is in error, explain it to your coach and leave it up to him or her to make the objection. Moving on means exactly that—don't let your mistake haunt you for the rest of the game. Don't beat yourself up over a mistake and don't pout over a call that doesn't go your way.

An important aspect of sportsmanship is keeping your head where it needs to be to give your best possible performance in practice or competition. Just as you would not continue to bring up a teammate's mistake, you need to extend yourself that same courtesy.

COACHES » Make sure you are setting the tone for your team in the way you respond to game officials and other teams. Some teams have a reputation throughout the league for being difficult, and that can affect the way an official is inclined to rule on an iffy call.

Whether or not that is fair, it can be true. What is even more potentially damaging is when the argumentative nature of a team extends to the relationships between teammates themselves. In order to combat this destructive behavior, make sportsmanship front and center for your players from day one. Make sure they understand your role as the one to lodge complaints, insist your athletes be respectful and polite toward *everyone* at games and meets, and show zero tolerance for the blame game among team members.

We often speak of sportsmanship in terms of how we as individuals treat others and respond to competitors, officials, coaches, and our own teammates. We often forget to think of sportsmanship in terms of how we deal with our own successes and failures as an athlete. It is important to celebrate our successes without becoming arrogant, and it is incredibly important to use our failures as stepping stones. We cannot beat ourselves up, although it is often easier to do that than to simply move on, especially when the stakes are high.

I vividly remember my first international competition. I had been paralyzed about a year-and-a-half prior and only out of high school for a few years. I was in Rio de Janeiro, Brazil, at the 2009 IPC Swimming Short Course World Championships. I had won a few gold medals so far in the competition, and expectations were high as I went into my 200m Individual Medley. I had so many mixed emotions. It was one of my weakest events but was also one for which I had been training incredibly hard, and all I wanted was to reach the podium. I still remember looking up at the scoreboard following my race and seeing my time and then a number 3 next to my name.

I had just made it onto the podium and would be bringing home a bronze medal in that event!

Moments after the race, as I was in the cool-down pool, I received word I had been disqualified on a turn. I was incredibly frustrated and mad at myself, wondering how in the world I could have made such a silly mistake at this level in my career. I ended up staying in the cool-down pool doing turn after turn at full speed, wasting an excessive amount of energy when I still had days of competition left.

I often think back to that day as a reminder mistakes happen; sometimes we fall and sometimes we fail. But no matter what, we must get back up and show the same grace to ourselves we do to our teammates and competitors. Sportsmanship doesn't just extend to others in our respective sports; it also extends to us.

TEAMWORK

A team's ability to work together at this level can absolutely make or break it. If the members of a team trust one another, they will work harder in practice because they feel driven to improve and will push harder in competition to make sure they are making a contribution to the team's overall success.

ATHLETES » Ask yourself what you are doing to promote trust on your team. Do you ever talk about a teammate behind her back? Do you give someone such a hard time that he might feel uncomfortable or even unsafe? Or do you stand up for your teammates and let them know you respect them and care about them, even if you don't always get along? Building trust is key to working together well.

Remember, too, there may be more than meets the eye going on in your teammates' personal lives. You may not know everything your fellow teammates are experiencing. They could be dealing with some very heavy or adult matters that are clouding their ability to keep their head in the game. If someone who is normally on top of things seems a little discombobulated one day, don't think you should call that person on the rug. Try to give your teammates the benefit of the doubt and extend them some grace. You would like the same done for you. If your coach brings someone in or benches another and you don't understand why, it may be that he or she is aware of something you're not. Don't let that affect you and your game.

COACHES >> Communication is key for building trust. Encourage your players to communicate openly with one another and with you, and do the same in return. This is true both on and off the field, on and off the court, and in or out of the pool. If you create a culture of honest, clear communication, players will know what is expected of them in practice, competition, and how they relate to one another.

Throughout high school, my swimming teammates were some of my closest friends. Unfortunately, I had to deal with some undesirable life circumstances during my high school years—health issues of a family member as well as health issues of my own. The one place I always felt comfort on the hardest days was the pool, and that had a lot to do with my teammates and coaches. Life brings with it challenges, adversity, and less-than-ideal circumstances; but when you are on the field, in the pool, or on the court, you should be able to escape from it all and just be a kid. Our team had its cliques; it had its drama—I think all teams have to work through that—but we also came together when it really mattered. We had pasta feeds before the end of the season. We made shirts and posters together. Those on varsity went to the JV championship to cheer for our teammates, and those on JV went to sectionals and state to cheer on the rest of the team. Part of what built such a strong culture of teamwork was the influence of our captains and coaches. They modeled leadership, which made the rest of us want to invest in our team as well.

Looking back, high school swimming was one of the most memorable times of my career. It is where I had the opportunity to build some of my closest friendships, grow as an individual, and learn the power of the sport. I often say, "you are only as good as the people you surround yourself with," and this is true in all aspects of life. Remember to be grateful to those who make up your team, from your teammates to your coaches to your parents and supporters. The power of a team is tremendous.

JOIN THE CONVERSATION!

For more stories and conversations with athletes and coaches, download the **COMPLETE ATHLETE** app!

PROFESSIONALISM

PROFESSIONALISM overlaps a great deal with sportsmanship at Level 3. The way an athlete conducts himself or herself after competition is every bit as important as conduct during it. It goes without saying a professional respects his or her competitors as well as the integrity of the game and follows all the rules and regulations governing competition. But an athlete's reaction to a win or loss also matters.

ATHLETES >> Imagine how deflating it would be if you just beat a rival who normally comes out on top and heard him or her say, "well, I just missed the wall on my flip turn" or, "my shoe came untied; that's the only reason I didn't keep up with you." Immediately, someone just tried to discredit your win, rather than admitting you happened to be the better athlete that day. Now imagine the tables are turned—is that sort of reaction your immediate response to a loss?

It's human nature to want to find someone or something to blame for the outcome if you lose a tough competition. By Level 3, however, you should be mature enough to keep that impulse in check. Any great competitor hates to lose, but a **COMPLETE ATHLETE** stands out from the pack by handling it with class. Instead of making excuses, congratulate the winners—and maybe even remind them you'll be coming for them next time!

But to write their victory off as a fluke looks petty and marks you as a poor sportsman. Don't put down or shame your teammates either if they are working hard but not performing up to your standards. That's not your job.

Likewise, accept wins gracefully. You have absolutely earned the right to celebrate—especially if you just outscored someone who normally beats you—but don't give in to the temptation to rub it in. One of the hallmarks of professionalism is maturity, and as hard as it is to stay in control of your emotions and reactions in big moments, a **COMPLETE ATHLETE** does just that.

Making an off-hand comment to a competitor is something that happens all the time in the higher levels of athletics, but it is something you rarely see from the best of the best. People who are truly confident in their abilities and understand that sports are about so much more than the win-loss tally don't feel the need to take others down.

In the 2016 Rio Olympics, Michael Phelps not only celebrated his teammates' wins but also didn't make excuses when he ended up in a three-way tie for silver, losing the gold to Joseph Schooling of Singapore. In fact, Phelps applauded Schooling and congratulated him on giving him such a tough race for silver, adding that this sort of increasing fierceness in competition is exactly what the sport should be about.

In Rio, I had an incredible race in one of my strongest events even though I didn't medal. I was feeling great about my time and what I had accomplished... until one of the medalists remarked in an accusatory tone, "what happened to you? You started strong, but then you just fell back." That one comment took me from feeling great to feeling deflated about my accomplishment. No, I had not won or medaled—I took fifth place—but I had gotten one of my lifetime-best times. That race was about so much more than a medal to me.

Perfect competitions almost never happen. In fact, there are only two races in my entire career where I would not change a single thing. Two. You may not have a perfect race or game, but odds are your competition didn't either. It comes down to who was the better athlete that day. Some days it will be you; some days it will not. There is no need to belittle someone else's performance, whether they beat you or whether you beat them. Have a filter between your brain and your mouth, and don't necessarily say everything you are thinking.

The mark of a true professional is someone who can lose —and win—with grace.

LEADERSHIP

At Level 3, natural leaders will begin to emerge as athletes become mature enough to take on **LEADERSHIP** roles. It is important to remember, however, the responsibility of leadership should not fall entirely on the shoulders of one athlete. Every person needs to take on a different role within the team. There will be times when the natural leader has a bad day. Other teammates need to be ready and willing to step up and carry some of that responsibility. Leaders understand a team is a partnership.

ATHLETES >> You are only as good as your team average, so you've got to be willing to help one another carry the load. The best leaders are the people who aren't going to ask anyone else to do the work they are not willing to do themselves.

Communicate clearly to your teammates you are some-one who is going to have their back both on and off the field. While you may not be close to all your teammates, they have to know that you are going to stand beside them on the court or in the rink no matter what. People will automatically respect someone they know they can trust. This is how leaders emerge in any setting, be it sports or politics—they are team members whom others feel will protect their interests.

It's not enough to say that you want to be a team leader; you have to give your teammates reason to believe that you will fight for them and overcome obstacles together. More so than the name on your jerseys, mutual trust is the glue holding you together as a team. Leadership is not about who posts the best stats or has the most impressive scholarship offers. If you strive to be a leader, you must respect the trust you have built with your teammates and not break it. It is important to realize leadership carries many roles and isn't about being the most popular player—it is about upholding your values and the values of your team through success and failure and being someone who respects the bond between every member of your team.

Your team is more than just the people who take the field with you; your broader team is the whole community of support, from your family and coaches to your teachers and neighbors. Too often, people concentrate only on how one or two athletes stand out as leaders for the way they perform in competition. But real leadership is much more and extends much further than the people on the roster.

When I was facing my new reality following my paralysis, it was my team—that larger community of people rooting and fighting for me—who helped me piece my life back together again. I had been the captain of my high school team, but now I needed to rely on the strength of other people while I figured out my new reality. I also came to understand how real leadership works; it's not about being the best competitor out there but about stepping up when needed. I witnessed some incredible leaders step up and help guide me and raise me up from my darkest hour. Surround yourself with a team that will fight for you and for whom you want to fight. These are the people who will lift you up when you fall.

Now, before every race, I remind myself of that incredible quote from the movie Any Given Sunday, *where Tony D'Amato (Al Pacino) says "That's what living is, the six inches in front of your face. Now I can't make you do it. You've got to look at the guy next to you, look into his eyes. Now I think you're gonna see a guy who will go that inch with you. You're gonna see a guy who will sacrifice himself for this team because he knows, when it comes down to it, you're gonna do the same for him. That's a team, gentlemen, and either we heal as a team or we will die as individuals."*

A leader is someone who remembers that and reminds others of it. If an athlete wants to be a leader, he or she needs to be someone who can recognize what is needed and is willing to rise to the occasion.

3.2 PREPARATION

Mentality is one of the most important aspects of **PREPARATION**, and, at Level 3, it becomes every bit as important as physical training. What an athlete puts in his or her body and how he or she exercises is significant, but without the mental component, the physical side won't count for much.

ATHLETES » Mentality is about more than being mentally present during practices and competitions. In high school, grit will begin to separate the good athletes from the great ones. Grit is hard to define and impossible to teach. It is something that can only be gained by experience; you can't learn it by reading about it in a book. Grit is the accumulation of year after year of choices to push through, the memory of what you've endured and what you've survived. Grit is the understanding your mind will give up before your body will. And the only way to develop it is by pushing past the voice that tells you to quit—the one that says you can't run another step, swim another stroke, or hold a pin for one more second.

4

PARENTS AND COACHES >> Athletes at this age are old enough to receive tough love. It's not really something you can (or should) do earlier because children are not emotionally mature enough to process the lessons in elementary or middle school. But once you reach high school, teenagers do not need to be babied in their training. There is a line, of course, but coaches play an important role in encouraging their athletes to keep pushing past the point where their mind plays tricks on them. The mind will quit before the body does, but athletes have to learn not to let it. Learning to push past that point of mental resistance is a key component of Navy SEAL training, and high school athletes who want to compete at elite levels need to start learning how to reach for that same place.

Without a doubt, some of the best races of my entire career have come when my body felt like toast, and I had to rely on my mind to overcome that.

When I was in high school, our team attended an annual swimming invitational early in the season. I remember always feeling sore as our coach put us through grueling workouts the week leading in, and as a result, my body felt as though it had been pushed to the max going into the meet. Yet I almost always racked up some of my best in-season times. As my career progressed, I found this pattern continued; some of my strongest races happened when I was forced to make it a competition of mental toughness.

That's what grit is: the ability to gut something out because you know your body is capable even though your mind disagrees and the experience of knowing this is true. If you power through and get your mind to a place where it is no longer sending you signals to give up, you will be infinitely more powerful than you ever imagined.

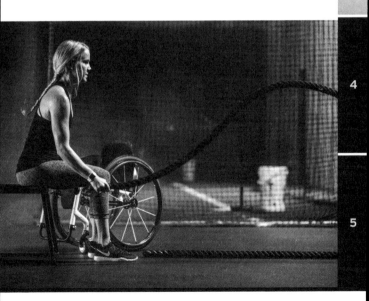

3.3 FITNESS

Building off the idea of mental toughness and fighting past physical discomfort, athletes need to understand the difference between good and bad fatigue. In Level 2, we talked about listening to the body in terms of figuring out its new capabilities and limitations as it changes. In Level 3, an athlete needs to be in-tune enough to know the difference between a body that is breaking down to build back up stronger versus a body that is overworked or broken to the point of serious strain or injury.

ATHLETES >> You need to be smart about how you prepare your body for competition, which means you need to continue focusing on using correct technique as you train. The number of repetitions you do or the amount you can bench press doesn't matter if your technique is wrong. Consider pursuing **FITNESS** opportunities outside your sport. By diversifying the ways you stretch your body, you can help prevent overuse injuries while still reaping the benefits of overall muscle development.

Most importantly, understand what is normal and what is not. After three days of intense training, your body will absolutely be sore. However, if you begin to feel more tired than seems reasonable and are still extremely sore after allowing your body at least 48 hours of rest and good nutrition, you may be breaking down your body in an unhealthy way. Any intense, acute pain in a bone or joint is a concern as well. By now, you should have a fairly good sense of what is normal for your body, and you should act accordingly with your coaches, parents, and a healthcare team to diagnose and treat any injury or concern. Prevention, however, should still be your primary goal.

COACHES » Make sure your athletes are smart about how they prepare their bodies for competition. Despite what you may be tempted to think, the end goal of fitness right now is still injury prevention rather than sheer, brute strength. Range of motion, mobility of joints, reaction time, etc., are more important than being the biggest/fastest/strongest athlete in terms of career prospects and longevity.

I've seen too many young athletes harm themselves by turning training into a competition. I get it: We are naturally competitive. That's just how we are wired. It's hard to resist going into the weight room and trying to out-lift your teammates—but do you really win in the long run if you tear a ligament and blow out your knee in the process? Allow yourself to navigate the fine line between mental toughness and pushing your body to the point of injury.

3.4 TECHNIQUE

Although the fundamentals of a sport should be second nature by this point, that doesn't mean they no longer matter. In fact, checking on **TECHNIQUE** periodically can help prevent injury, improve performance, and even help an athlete snap out of a slump.

ATHLETES AND COACHES » You may believe by the time you've reached high school there is not a whole lot to be gained by studying the basic techniques of your sport —but nothing could be further from the truth. Even though fundamentals probably won't be your main focus right now, you should run a technique check on yourself periodically (or encourage your athletes to do so) to make sure bad habits haven't crept in. As your body continues to grow, strengthen, and change, you need to make sure it is still able to master the basic forms of your sport.

You are never too old or experienced to focus on technique. As sports science changes, sports can change, which means athletes need to adapt too. Consider the changes in the construction of running tracks in the last 30 years, what we have learned about water flow in a pool, or how starting blocks have developed. With each change comes new ways to advance our technique. The more we learn about how the human body works, the more we learn about how to effectively utilize our energy. We have seen cleats advance, the way speed suits for skiing have changed, the redesign of materials in competition suits for swimming— all of which have had a direct impact on competition. The changing shape of techniques, equipment, and materials all reflect new advances in sports science, from how we train to our understanding of muscle recovery. Methods I used in high school are now out of date as the sport has evolved over the years.

Allow yourself to find a passion for learning about your sport and invest yourself in studying the latest advances. This doesn't mean you should chase every trend or fad, but it does mean you should be willing to adapt and dedicate yourself to mastering and re-mastering the fundamentals. What you practice in training becomes second nature in competition. Always make sure you never get sloppy with your technique in training in an effort to take shortcuts. Be mentally present and execute proper technique during practice. If you don't, how can you expect your body to execute proper technique during competition?

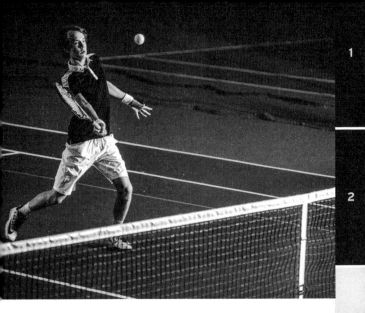

3.5 LIFESTYLE

In Level 2, we discussed how important it is to find the right balance between academics, sports, and other commitments. The stakes are much higher now as every grade counts toward a student's overall GPA and class ranking. Coaches and scouts may also be watching to see how an athlete performs both on and off the field. Add in the pressures of academic eligibility to play as well as qualification for recruiting showcases and college, and the need for balance becomes even greater.

FAMILY

FAMILY plays a key role in finding balance. Everything at home makes a difference in helping a student-athlete stay in line. A family calendar, showing up to games, knowing when to offer advice and when to simply offer support—any and all of these provide the structure teenagers need as they navigate through the difficult choices and pressures of high school on their way to becoming young adults.

ATHLETES >> Your family is the support group that will help you reach the goals you have in place for your life, so make sure there is an open line of communication between yourself, your parents, and your siblings. Your family—whatever it looks like—should comprise your biggest supporters, but make sure you are returning the favor by reciprocating that support rather than just absorbing all of it for yourself.

PARENTS >> At this point, teachers and coaches are probably really putting on the pressure, and students can easily feel overwhelmed not only by the day-to-day tasks, but also by the major, life-altering decisions they are facing: where to go to college, finding a second choice if the first does not accept them, choosing a major, etc. A parent's job right now is to help guide those decisions but also remind the student not everything has to be decided immediately. Transferring to a different university may be an option if one doesn't feel like a good fit after the first year or the student ultimately decides to go somewhere else. It's OK to be undeclared on day one of college. These choices matter, but they will not make or break your child's life while still in high school. If your children seem stressed by these pressures, remind them they are still kids even as they begin to face adult decisions.

COACHES >> At Level 3, coaches may actually spend more facetime with students during the week than parents do, so it is important to realize the impact and influence you have on keeping student-athletes on the right path. Remind your players that, just as you need them to be mentally present at practice, you also need them to be every bit as present in the classroom and with their families. This way they will have the academic readiness and emotional support necessary to maintain a healthy balance. The best way for a team to be successful is for every player to be a **COMPLETE ATHLETE**.

Above all else, your family should be your No. 1 priority. I learned at a young age when the going gets tough, your family will always have your back. As we talk about becoming a **COMPLETE ATHLETE***, remember it isn't always about life going perfectly. It is in those imperfect moments that we must allow ourselves to rely on our loved ones and family members to help us pull ourselves up. High school may bring challenges for some, while for others it may seem like a breeze. Regardless of your experience, remember your family is there to help you navigate the highs and lows all the same. Always be mindful to support your siblings, and your parents in their own endeavors as well.*

ACADEMICS

In high school, **ACADEMICS** matter more than they ever have before. The skills and knowledge gained will not only prepare the student-athlete for life, but also determine eligibility for playing time as well as college scholarships. In other words, high school grades matter in the short-term, mid-term, *and* long-term.

ATHLETES » Those time management skills you honed

in middle school will now prove invaluable as you juggle a more intense course load as well as more intense practice sessions and perhaps personal training time. If you plan to take AP or dual-enrollment courses for college credit, life will become even more challenging. You will likely be forced to make some tough decisions during those weeks when it seems like every teacher and coach has turned up the heat at once. What if you are faced with the need to stay late after school for tutoring, which will result in being late for practice?

Remember to focus on what makes you a better person, not just a better athlete. Mastering a formula in calculus may not seem more important than what is going on with your team, but your performance in the classroom has a lasting impact on your overall GPA. It affects everything from your class rank to college scholarships to college programs you may want to apply to in the future. Also, your education is what will set you up for all future success after sports. This doesn't just apply to core curriculum classes either. Does taking part in art or drama make you better? Does playing an instrument or studying an additional foreign language make you more well-rounded and bring you joy? If so, you need to allow yourself some time and energy for these pursuits so your life (and your brain) is dedicated to more than just school and sports. With that in mind, the decision to spend a little extra time in tutoring should become a little easier to make.

Under all this pressure, you may feel as though you are fighting a losing battle. Not everyone is a straight-A student. Academic success comes much easier for some people than others. If you fail a test or struggle during a particular unit, *do not despair!* You can absolutely bounce back from one tough semester if you apply yourself to raising those grades going forward. What is more concerning to college coaches is evidence of a pattern of poor academic performance, or evidence you are struggling more than you should with time management or maintaining school-sport balance. Thus, don't let a C-minus on your English essay make you think you need to give up on your athletic dreams; just know you have identified an area where you may need to spend a little more time studying to master the material and commit to doing so going forward.

PARENTS >> While it is ultimately up to your child whether he or she puts in the necessary work for academic success, it is still essential you emphasize best choices at home. Make sure your child feels as supported in schoolwork as on the field. For parents whose child is naturally an honor roll student, this may seem obvious. But for those kids who have always found success in athletics much easier than success in the classroom, this can be a tougher balance to find. Any athlete whose sole focus is the sport *will* plateau and *will* burn out. That is just the reality of what a body and emotions can handle. Truthfully, an athletic career can only last so long before injury or retirement brings it to an end. Education will last longer than knee joints, so make sure you are putting what will benefit your child the most in the long-term first.

COACHES >> It may be painful to bench a player for academic ineligibility, but your goal as a coach needs to be the teen's long-term development as a person outside the sports world. If a parent informs you he or she is requiring a child to miss practice or games until grades improve, you need to support that decision rather than undermine it.

During my sophomore year of high school, I had the incredible opportunity to tour Italy with my school choir over spring break. The only glitch was rehearsals started in the fall during swim season and conflicted, at times, with training. My parents always encouraged my sisters and me to enjoy other extracurricular activities outside of our sport, and this was an opportunity I felt I couldn't pass up. I learned that, although my swimming was important, it was also important for me to explore other opportunities as a student-athlete. Learning to balance our devotion to sport while also allowing ourselves to experience life outside of sport is an important skill to learn early on. This balancing act is one that becomes an art as we continue in our athletic careers to the collegiate level and maybe even onto the professional stage. It can help a great deal to consult the people in whom we trust, including our parents and coaches.

That trip to Italy proved to be such an incredible opportunity to explore a different part of the world, learn the rich cultural history of different cities all over Italy, and to sing in the St. Peter's Basilica during an Easter week service. Those are memories that were truly once in a lifetime and, for me, were worth the sacrifice. Often, as athletes, we find ourselves at a crossroads with various opportunities, and though these are very personal decisions, remember that being a **COMPLETE ATHLETE** means allowing yourself to grow, not just as an athlete but also as a person.

SOCIAL LIFE

One of the major choices Level 3 athletes make is whether to compete with their high school team or to commit solely to competing in elite club sports. Some states allow student-athletes to do both; others have much tighter restrictions on whether an athlete can compete or even train in both venues simultaneous. Ultimately, the decision is a deeply personal one and only the student-athlete and their parents really know what the best choice is in terms of their future goals. One thing to consider, however, is how much the student-athlete is willing to sacrifice in terms of a **SOCIAL LIFE** in order to participate in the sport.

ATHLETES >> By now, you already understand sacrifice is part of success, no matter what venue. Maintaining a social life in high school can be tricky for athletes because so much of your time outside of school and homework is dominated by your sport. This is one of the areas where knowing your values becomes especially important. Do you want to go pro, do you hope to compete in college but have no ambitions beyond that, or do you plan to end your athletic career with high school? You should consider this question carefully and weigh the implications of each as you make your choices.

No matter what you decide, however, it is important you allow yourself some kind of social life outside of athletics. Social interaction with a variety of people and in a variety of environments is essential for healthy emotional development. Even if you decide you want to make your professional ambitions your No. 1 goal, you still need to allow yourself some time to make friends, blow off steam, and grow as a person who is more than just one dimension.

1

2

3

4

5

For me, competing as a member of my high school team never seemed to be a question; it was automatic. Growing up, I watched my two older sisters compete for our high school team; I knew the coaches since I was a little kid; I swam on a club team where it was encouraged to swim for your high school. Honestly, I don't know if I knew anyone from our club team who didn't choose to swim for their high school team. (It is important to note, depending on the program that you compete for year-round, there may need to be some discussions on how to best manage the change or what the eligibility rules are for high school competition.)

I can say I would never trade my high school swimming experience. Competing as an Eagan Wildcat taught me so much more than sport. It taught me about the deep level of love and respect I had for the sport. It taught me about being a part of a team in a sport that is so often seen *as an individual sport. It taught me about school pride and spirit, and gave me that connection to the greater community as I represented Eagan.*

At this age, it is important to take your athletic career seriously, especially depending on what your goals for the sport may be. However, it is also important to remember that you are a kid and you don't get these years back. Being devoted to your sport and making sacrifices are part of being an athlete, and it is important to learn how to have that level of devotion and drive toward your goals, but also how to keep it within reason. Remember that balance is just as important as anything else. Don't give up on being a kid too young; you have the rest of your life to be an adult.

As I look back to my high school years, I can say with full confidence if it weren't for my years as a high school athlete, I wouldn't have returned to the water following my paralysis. High school swimming is what has laid the foundation for the rest of my career. Just as competing as a member of Team USA has become a hugely influential part of my life, swimming as a high school athlete was just as influential for me as a person. There is no way to replace that experience.

ROLE MODEL

At Level 3, athletes begin transitioning from having **ROLE MODELS** to being role models. This doesn't mean high school athletes don't still have role models themselves—they can and should! But it does mean teenagers should be conscious of the example they are setting as they become the very people they once looked up to themselves.

ATHLETES » If you have younger siblings, you may have already been a role model to younger children for several years. If not, now is the time when you may begin to notice elementary and middle school kids on your club team or in your community watching you carefully and even starting to imitate your words and actions. The older kids in a group tend to be the "cool kids" whom the younger ones try to emulate. Whether you want to be a role model or not, you don't really get a whole lot of say in the matter. Make sure you are acting in such a way that makes you worthy of respect.

COACHES » Remind your players they have a special responsibility to make good choices and be good examples to younger kids who are watching them. The way they handle wins and losses, deal with adversity, exhibit work ethic, display their attitude both on and off the field of play—all of these factors matter more than just face value. They also have the weight of setting an example for someone else. It is a big transition to go from idolizing older teammates to becoming the hometown heroes themselves, but part of being an athlete means people will be watching. Encourage your athletes— individually and as a team—to think seriously about the kind of role models they want to be.

While you will begin to be a role model for younger athletes as you get older, you will still need your own role models. Some of the biggest role models in my life have been the people closest to me, from my two older sisters to my parents and coaches. I wasn't a child with a larger-than-life hero; my childhood role models were my parents. They were the people I watched go through life, handling its adversities and joys, twists and turns. I watched as they gracefully dealt with the circumstances life threw their way and felt supported as they encouraged my sisters and me to chase after our dreams. Role models aren't always famous athletes or individuals. They are sometimes the very people in front of us on a daily basis. And just as those individuals may serve as your biggest role models, remember you may soon do the same for someone else.

LIVING YOUR SPORT

For an athlete to compete successfully in high school, he or she must set personal goals for achievement and growth along the way. One of the most significant aspects of **LIVING YOUR SPORT** is learning how to incorporate goal-setting into *every aspect* of life.

ATHLETES >> By reaching this level, you have proven you can set goals and put in the work to achieve them. Whether breaking a certain speed with your pitch, finishing a race under a certain time, or mastering a specific skill, you have advanced this far because you put your mind to becoming better at your sport. Now, in addition to your athletic goals, you need to ask yourself if you have put the same kind of dedication and hard work into setting and achieving goals regarding who you want to be outside the world of sports. What are your ultimate goals for life beyond competition?

When I talk to high school athletes, I am frequently asked these two questions: "How do you set new goals?" and "When do you know to reassess your goals?"

What I explain to those students is there are three kinds of goals we can set for ourselves: short-term, long-term, and the-sky-is-the-limit. Short-term goals are things we hope to achieve in any given day, week, or month; they are specific and have clearly defined time constraints. Long-term goals are what we hope to see come to pass over the course of a season or year; they can be specific in terms of the outcome, but they are usually more general in terms of overall experience or cumulative improvement. The-sky-is-the-limit goals are the ones where we allow ourselves to be kids again and put the craziest, most amazing, most optimistic, most ambitious goals before ourselves and say, "Why not?"

Many athletes find goal-setting challenging because we are naturally competitive and don't like to lose. Thus, we do not set goals we might not reach. As a result, we often cheat ourselves by setting "safe" goals rather than writing down goals that scare us a little.

Maybe it's because we've been told we're not good enough or we've let ourselves believe greatness belongs to someone else. This is a big sticking point for a lot of Level 3 athletes.

In high school, I got a C in public speaking; less than 5 years later, I spoke before the UN General Assembly for a TEDx event. I now travel the country as a motivational speaker for everyone from school groups to major corporations. In an average year, I speak in front of roughly 25,000 people.

When I was paralyzed, I was told I would never walk again, and in some ways, that is true—I will never walk entirely with my own strength and volition again. However, thanks to advances in engineering and healthcare, my team at the Mayo Clinic in Rochester, Minnesota, helped create a set of full-length leg braces and a device called an "Up and About" that allows me short periods of upright mobility with the help of forearm crutches. Thanks to these amazing braces and countless hours with my physical therapists, I was even able to walk down the aisle at my wedding.

Rather than allowing someone else to define "possible" for me, I decided to pursue my own goals. I have learned over my life the only limits we have are the ones we create. I can offer Level 3 athletes no more important advice than this: Do not be afraid to set ambitious or even seemingly impossible goals. So what if you don't reach exactly where you were aiming? The only true failure is not giving yourself the chance to attempt to reach your dreams.

IN LEVEL 4

Athletes have developed a solid foundation of skill and sportsmanship in their careers; now is the time to realize the power of community more than ever. It is important athletes represent not just themselves but their larger community with grace and integrity.

An open mind is a major component of success at Level 4. College is the first time most athletes will ever move away from home, and this huge life change can leave student-athletes feeling scared, excited, overwhelmed, or empowered—or maybe all of these emotions at once.

4.1 ATTITUDE

A new Level 4 athlete will likely be facing numerous new situations all at once: living in a dorm, having a roommate (who may or may not be a fellow athlete), a different type of class structure, an entirely new schedule, and a new team. An athlete who is willing to enter into this new way of living, studying, and training with a **POSITIVE ATTITUDE** and an open mind is far more likely to adapt and thrive than one who resists these changes at every turn.

RESPECT

RESPECT for the new team, coaching staff, and broader athletic and academic community is essential, as is respect for the school a student-athlete now represents. It is worth revisiting Levels 1 and 2 to review the fundamentals of developing and exhibiting respect for coaches and teammates; this may seem obvious, but it may not be quite as automatic as one might think.

Additionally, it is important to remember self-respect and personal values, which were discussed in Level 3. College can bring with it a lot of wonderful experiences, but it can also present a number of opportunities to make poor choices or decisions that go against a **COMPLETE ATHLETE**'s core beliefs.

Athletes must respect their values as they work on becoming open-minded. There are some areas where it is beneficial to be willing to try new things. In other areas, it is better to stick with the beliefs that make you *you*.

ATHLETES >> Entering college can be a major shock to your training system, playing style, and your sense of camaraderie. Your new coaching staff may have a completely different style and philosophy from your previous coaches with whom you may have trained for many years. Although you probably researched your new coach and his or her methods before deciding to play for a team, adapting to new kind of leadership or learning a new position can be challenging.

In fact, you may even feel as though you are being disloyal to your old coach or old team in doing so. Don't worry—these are perfectly natural feelings. Nonetheless, keep your focus on your *team now* and allow yourself to broaden your knowledge of the game and execution of techniques according to your current team's needs. Remember your new team cares about your success and wants you to excel as much as your old team did, so don't be afraid to adapt to new demands.

Be sure to respect your new school as well. You are now part of a tradition that stretches back far beyond you; the way you act as an extension of that college and its athletics program affects its reputation. Keep that in mind as you are faced with everyday decisions.

Since you are surrounded by a new set of teammates, remember they don't necessarily know you and your core values, so they may not be able to hold you accountable in the same way your high school team did. This is why respect for yourself and your beliefs is so important, especially in the first semester or two of college. You may not have the same support system around you to help steer you back if you go off path. Make sure you are true to who you really are, both on and off the field.

PARENTS >> Whether your child is 30 minutes from home or a four-hour plane ride away, the first semester of college—and beyond—can be a stressful time for you both. Many parents have to fight the urge to be the dreaded "helicopter parents," those who continue to take an overly involved role as their children pass into adulthood. Other parents are ready to celebrate being empty nesters the moment their youngest child goes away to school and hardly ever call. Parents must fight the urge to go to either extreme. Yes, your child is now a young adult and needs to learn how to live independently, but he or she also needs to be assured your love and concern for them has not changed. You won't be able to be there when your child is sick, experiences major heartbreak, faces a moral dilemma, or feels alone, but you can check in with phone calls, emails, and cards now and then. Remind your college students of their core values and how to respect them; tell them how proud you are of them and their accomplishments—especially on days when they feel the lowest. Remember, too, that your attitude still matters at this level.

I remember the first few nights after my parents dropped me off at school. I went to Gardner-Webb University midyear, as a transfer student, and after a few days of having my parents help me settle in, they left for the airport to fly home to Minnesota. I still remember looking around my dorm room realizing the time had finally come for me to be on my own—and as exciting as it was, it also brought a sense of homesickness. That day was three weeks before my one-year anniversary of becoming paralyzed, which made it even harder. At this age, there is so much natural change in a young adult's life, and I felt all the pressures of trying to find my calling and my purpose while also learning how to navigate life on my own for the first time since my paralysis.

It is natural to miss home; it is also natural to have times when you forget about the world back home because you are so engrossed in your school life. Whichever side you find yourself on, always remember where you came from. For me, that sense of belonging was what helped me branch out on my own in college. As we talk about respect in Level 4, remember above all to respect yourself and the values you hold. If you can manage that, the rest will fall into place. If you remember where you came from, you will, in turn, remain grounded as you navigate this new chapter in your life.

SPORTSMANSHIP

By Level 4, good **SPORTSMANSHIP** should be second nature, which is important because now there are going to be more eyes on an athlete than ever before.

ATHLETES » You may find your matches, meets, or games televised now or at least available in a streaming format online. You may even find yourself giving post-match interviews. Although a good sportsman or sportswoman exhibits respectful behavior even when the cameras aren't on, the stakes are even higher when your visibility is much greater.

A **COMPLETE ATHLETE** should be a tough but gracious competitor. Offer a hand to someone you just tackled. Take a knee when a member of the other team is injured. Don't hang on the rim an extra few seconds after a dunk. Don't throw your cap and goggles on the pool deck if you lose, and don't taunt your competitors if you win. Remember you represent a school, a tradition, a program, an alumni base, and a community that is bigger than yourself.

There will be competitors who trash talk you; don't respond. There will be rival fans who try to get a rise out of you; don't give them the satisfaction. There will be online trolls who try to taunt you; don't let them get into your head. There may even be members of the media who want to goad you into saying or doing something incendiary for the sake of a story; don't indulge them. Whether you win or lose, the first thing you should always do in an interview is congratulate the other team or opponent. There are more people watching you than ever, and the name on the front of your jersey matters more than the name on the back of it.

I still remember my first meet as a Gardner-Webb Running Bulldog, putting on that cap and the pride I felt representing a community so much larger than myself. I instantly felt connected to my college community because they were some of the first people in my life who truly embraced me following my injury. After my paralysis, everyone in my life knew me as the Mallory I was before. Thus, as I was trying to grieve what had happened and learn how to navigate this new life, so were my family and friends. However, at Gardner-Webb, not a single person knew me before my injury, and it became the fresh start I needed to find my way through that time in my life and learn how to move on.

Multiple times throughout my season at Gardner-Webb, I was on the receiving end of incredible sportsmanship as others took the time to extend grace and support by offering a helping hand when I needed it most. That was one of the most vulnerable times in my life, and in my brief time as a collegiate athlete before turning pro, the sportsmanship of so many in the community helped me through.

We must remember when on the field of play that life extends beyond it. We must constantly challenge ourselves to view our teammates and competitors as fellow human beings. I understand as much as the next person the inner competitive drive that kicks in come competition. I am not saying you have to chat it up with your competitors prior to a game or race; however, you can still show respect. At this stage of your career, your actions are not only a direct reflection of who you are but also a direct reflection of the greater community you represent.

There is an expression: "People may not remember exactly what you did or what you said, but they will always remember how you made them feel." As you grow older, the wins and losses won't seem to matter anymore, but the person you choose to be on and off the court will always matter. Be a sportsman and sportswoman of integrity, one of respect, and one who pays tribute to the name on the front of their jersey more than the name on the back.

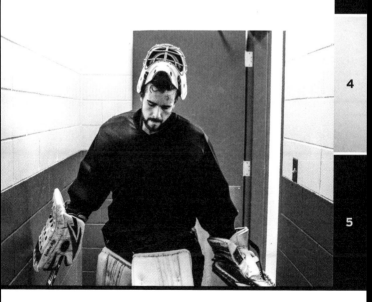

TEAMWORK

Your team is like a family in college. While teams at Level 3 feel very close, the closeness takes on a whole new dimension at Level 4. Athletes will spend the majority of their time outside class training and traveling with their teammates, along with the added component of living together in the dorms or campus housing. The way you interact together outside of practice and competition will almost certainly bleed over into the way you interact on the court or on the ice. This new level of proximity and intimacy means mutual trust and respect become more essential than ever.

ATHLETES >> One of the biggest adjustments faced by student-athletes entering college for the first time is new teammates that were once rivals. Hopefully, you conducted yourself in a way that there are no personal grudges between you, but it may require a bit of a shift to start viewing past competitors as friends and allies now. One way to forge a new relationship is to focus on your respect for this former rival as an athlete. The underlying admiration you may have for his or her technique or talent can be the basis of a new relationship as you figure out together how to build the trust necessary to benefit your shared team.

JOIN THE CONVERSATION!
Be a team player—join your teammates in the **COMPLETE ATHLETE** app!

You are one another's support system. In the absence of parents, siblings, or maybe even lifelong friends, your team members become the ones who lift you up, encourage you, push you when you need it, and carry you when things get rough. Because of this, it is imperative you be the kind of teammate you'd like to have. Bring food to the dorm when a teammate is sick; offer a ride to the airport if someone has to fly home for an emergency. Do the little and big things for each other that family normally would. The trust this creates is invaluable to the way you will function in competition.

PROFESSIONALISM

As mentioned before, a Level 4 student-athlete represents much more than just himself or herself. The student-athlete is part of a program with a history, a school with a pedigree of reputation, and a community of alumni and supporters. Athletes at every level represent their school or program, but at Level 4, as the recipient of a full or partial scholarship, the student must represent it in a professional manner. Even if the student is a walk-on or plays for a D-III school where there are no scholarships, he or she should still take pride in being part of a team that bears the name of the school and must act accordingly.

ATHLETES >> The way you uphold both your personal values *and* the values of your program—both on and off campus—is part of **PROFESSIONALISM**. For example, if you are caught underage drinking at a party, how does this reflect on both you and your team as a whole? All it takes is one person to make an irresponsible, dangerous, or criminal decision, and the entire program can be damaged or even jeopardized.

As a student-athlete, you should respect the greater community you represent. Respecting yourself, your family, your team, your program, and your community is crucial to the professionalism of a student-athlete. College is an incredible time in your life. You have the opportunity to meet new people, live on your own (probably for the first time), and establish yourself as an adult. But remember: with extra opportunities come more responsibilities.

How you carry yourself and what you say and do all reflect not only yourself but also the greater community you represent. Do so with pride and respect. Sometimes you have to sit back and ask yourself if it is really worth it. Is a night out at the bar when you are underage worth it in the long run? Are you willing to jeopardize not only your own reputation but also the reputation of the community you represent? Be smart. Think before you react on the field of play. Think before you speak in an interview or on social media. Think before you act off the field of play in social situations. To be a great athlete, you must be willing to think like a great athlete, whether in your social life, dealing with pressure in completion, or reacting to wins and losses. You must carry yourself with integrity in all situations.

LEADERSHIP

By Level 4, everyone should be mature enough to be a team leader, and most players probably *were* a captain or leader on their Level 3 team. This creates several interesting dynamics. It can be difficult for some athletes to make the transition back to being a junior member of the team. While there may sometimes be a bit of competition for power, much more significant is the fact that almost every member is equipped to step into a **LEADERSHIP** role when the need arises. Leaders can emerge throughout the season or even during a game or meet. Everyone's main concern should be a willingness to fill any role to help the team succeed.

ATHLETES » Know when to step up and when to step down. Be ready when you are called upon to provide your team with perspective, motivation, and even discipline. Just because you may be an underclassman does not mean you will never make a significant contribution to your team's shared success by taking the reins.

Conversely, be aware of your own limits and don't be afraid to ask for help or too proud to step aside in moments when you feel unqualified to lead. Find a balance between a willingness to lead and a willingness to be led by others who are older and more experienced.

By Level 4, you and most of your teammates have probably had some form of leadership role, whether as high school team captain or maybe even as a coach to younger athletes. At this point in your career, one of the best forms of leadership you can exhibit is stepping back from leadership when you realize you are not qualified for a particular role.

I have been on countless teams where we had individuals who saw themselves as leaders purely based on their popularity with teammates; unfortunately, popularity doesn't make you a good leader. Sometimes the best leaders are the ones who know their limits and step down because they recognize they are not currently in a place to lead. Make sure to know your strengths and weaknesses, and do not jeopardize the success of your team based on your desire to lead.

 **PREPARATION**

As discussed in previous levels, everything impacts the way an athlete performs, from dietary choices to sleep schedules to methods of dealing with stress. An athlete does not cease to be an athlete when he or she leaves the gym, pool, rink, or track; every decision made throughout the day influences the next one. Every choice a student-athlete makes is part of his or her **PREPARATION**.

Furthermore, as the stakes are higher than ever, grit becomes an even more essential part of training and performance. All the mental toughness you have been building will come into play and often becomes the deciding factor between two equally talented competitors.

ATHLETES >> Because everything you do impacts your sport and your readiness, make sure you are taking optimal steps to prepare your body for practice or competition. Be aware of everything you put in your body and how you treat it during "off" time. If you are tempted to stay out late at a party on Friday night but have an early practice Saturday morning, take an extra second to ask yourself if it is worth it.

Additionally, utilize the resources available to you. Most colleges have a wealth of resources available to student-athletes, including dietitians, physical therapists, academic advisors, and tutors. These specialists are part of your new community—they are members of your broader team. Their main concern is helping you prepare as effectively as possible, but they can't do their jobs unless you reach out to them.

Part of preparation is maintaining a mentality of mindful and intentional practice as well as the grit discussed in Level 3. Sports psychologists and good old self-discipline can play a huge role in helping you keep your mental game sharp.

Lean on your community—it is amazing how successful we can be in numbers. I have always said I don't believe we are meant to go through life alone, which is why we have family members, friends, teammates, loved ones, and communities. Lean on them! Sports are about so much more than mere physical performance. Make sure you are relying on your broader team and community to help you with the other components: your nutrition, mental and emotional well-being, and academics.

In my own career, I have learned physical preparation eventually becomes the easiest part as an athlete. We know how to push our bodies, and by this stage in the game, we know what it takes physically. The mental and emotional component to sport is one that is often the trickiest and one that can flip like a switch, even for the best. Social pressures seem to conflict with your schedule, voices seem to doubt your capabilities when you get run down and tired—these are very real struggles for Level 4 and 5 athletes, and I have dealt with them many times. It can feel as though you are always sacrificing for your sport but not always seeing it translate into success the way you would like. I have experienced plenty of "ruts" in my own career: times of doubt, uncertainty, and temptation toward distractions. This is where your community comes in. In these times, lean on coaches, teammates, family, loved ones—those you trust most to keep you on track.

To help yourself through these ups and downs, rely on community around you and establish a routine that works for you. Mental preparation and training is just as important, if not more so at times, as physical preparation. For me, I write quotes in my locker, on my water bottle—anywhere I can see them. I consciously remind myself why I am doing this and what I am working toward. I also rely on my parents and my husband, the very people who know me to my core and know my dreams, hopes, and desires. On days when I am mentally and emotionally spent, they help me keep going.

On race day, if I go into the ready room (which is where we report anywhere from 15 to 30 minutes before a national or international race) with any doubt, then I might as well not show up in the first place. The ready room—that place where you wait during the moments right before competition—is the biggest mind game you will ever play as an athlete. In these moments, you need to rely on your days, months, and years of mental preparation. Create your pre-competition routine. Practice it, envision it, and then on race day—execute. My routine is much more mental than physical because I have found what works for me. Whether racing at a collegiate conference meet or the Paralympic Games, I always find my parents in the stands from the pool deck. Right before I race, I look up to them and see my mom give me a thumbs-up that she seals with a kiss. At that moment, I know I am ready; my preparations are done. Before every race at the Rio 2016 Games, I saw my parents, my fiancé (now husband), and my coach in the stands as I sat on the starting block, and that was how I knew I was ready. These people, together, are a symbol reminding me of what I have done to get to that moment; they remind me—although it will be just me, seven other competitors, and that black line in a matter of seconds— that I am not alone. They are with me every stroke, and knowing that is the best preparation there is.

Lean on your community. Let them guide you when you feel lost. Let them celebrate your triumphs by your side. With them, you will always find your way and be ready come competition day. That moment of clarity, that moment of readiness before a competition or race—that doesn't just happen. It comes with years of focusing on your mental, emotional, and physical preparation. And when you finally get there, when you finally experience that feeling right before competition, that is when magic happens.

4.3 FITNESS

In addition to helping athletes prepare, the wellness team at a college or university wants to help athletes achieve and maintain **FITNESS**. Because competition is much more intense, the risk of injury is also greater. A university's wellness team and other healthcare advisors are invested in helping athletes prevent injuries and heal from them in the best way possible. This requires full cooperation from the athlete. In other words, insisting on playing through an overuse injury, refusing proper recovery time for a concussion, or re-entering competition before healing can endanger both an athlete's short- and long-term health.

Additionally, college marks the end of many competitors' athletic careers. While a number of student-athletes go on to coach or play in rec teams or community leagues, their ambitions do not extend to playing professionally. This means that college is often their final chance to push toward those career goals.

ATHLETES › As a Level 4 student-athlete, you will probably have more resources available to you than ever before. From trainers to sports psychologists to team chaplains, you will have resources available for every aspect of physical, mental, and spiritual fitness. Make sure you take advantage of this! College is a time when many athletes see the greatest boost in their abilities and greatest drop in their times due to physical and emotional growth coinciding with a wealth of resources. Don't miss the opportunity to use these resources to their fullest potential as you seek to maximize your athletic talent!

TECHNIQUE

With more training resources available than ever before, some of the most valuable are the video and sports science. A chance to break down **TECHNIQUE** with a coach who can provide a fresh set of eyes allows student-athletes to analyze and perfect their technique like never before.

ATHLETES › Once again, open-mindedness will prove essential in maximizing your Level 4 experience. You will be doing yourself a major disservice if you show up at college too set in your ways to trust your new coach. Of course, you will always respect and appreciate what your old coach did to lay the foundation for you to reach your current level, but now is the time to try new methods to help build upon that foundation. Your new coach likely recruited you and certainly wants to see you succeed; be willing to re-examine your technique, learn different tricks, or master new equipment or technologies that have recently emerged in your sport to continue growing.

Technique was an ever-evolving process for me as a Level 4 athlete. After becoming paralyzed at 18 and then returning to the sport of swimming, I found myself having to break down my strokes and go back to the basics. No longer having the use of my legs or the lower part of my core proved difficult, and as a result, forced me to have a much deeper level of respect for technique. It was amazing what stepping back and breaking down my strokes to the basics did for me as a swimmer. At this stage in our career, it is easy to be stubborn when it comes to our technique. We may believe our current technique is adequate. After all, it got us this far. Why fix what isn't broken? But breaking down our technique and keeping an open mind may allow us to tap into new potential we didn't even know we had, not to mention help prevent injuries.

It was amazing to me how many muscles I took for granted in my body and how many technical aspects of the sport I ignored prior to my paralysis. Instead, I had simply allowed the power from my legs to mask. As soon as I was no longer able to kick, I realized how crucial core stability and strength was to the alignment of my body in the water. I began playing with where my hands entered the water to maximize propulsion in the water and overall efficiency. I even learned that by utilizing my body in certain positions I could maintain control of areas I don't have function in while using what I do have to maximize efficiency. The biggest key to technical work in athletics is you cannot be stubborn; you must always be open to learning and stay in tune with your body throughout the process.

I have tweaked, adapted, and completely changed my technique on multiple occasions, and although every time has been a process of trial and error, in the long run it has allowed me to reach new heights as an athlete.

4.5 LIFESTYLE

Level 4 is all about change, and your **LIFESTYLE** is no exception. At Level 4, an athlete is going to be faced with a number of major changes, and now is an important time to begin asking questions about what life as an adult —away from home and apart from family—is going to look like. While this is a period for tremendous personal growth and independence, it is also a time when many young adults secretly worry about how they will manage and who they will become. Community plays an essential role in equipping student-athletes to conquer these fears so they can succeed and thrive in college.

FAMILY

FAMILY takes on a new role when an athlete moves away from home. It is still a foundational part of a student-athlete's community, but the relationships within will begin to change—and usually in positive ways. Even students who were eager to get out on their own in August are almost always incredibly excited to come home for the first big break (usually Thanksgiving). There is a whole new appreciation for home-cooked meals, laundry that doesn't require a roll of quarters, the old bedroom, and the many comforts of home.

ATHLETES >> You will probably come to appreciate your parents in entirely new ways during your first semester at college; swallow your pride and tell them. It is also important to make sure you stay connected with your siblings. Even though you are experiencing countless new things and making a new group of friends who will stand in for family when they can't be there, don't forget the people at home. Older siblings will want to hear from you to know how you are adapting; they may also be able to offer you useful advice. Younger siblings probably view you with a sense of awe—even if you didn't always get along when you were living under the same roof.

Make sure to reach out to them and let them know they are still a vital part of your life. As important as it is to invest yourself into developing meaningful relationships in your new community, don't just let the old ones go—they were instrumental in getting you to where you are now!

PARENTS >> Enjoy this new stage of parenting, where you can begin to take on more of a friend role to your child. Up to this point, it has been necessary to keep a

firm line between being parents and friends. You now can begin to let those lines blur a little as your child moves toward adulthood. Make sure they know you will always be their biggest fan and loudest cheerleader, no matter how old or how big a star they become!

ACADEMICS

ACADEMICS are first and foremost the reason why a student-athlete attends college. As tempting as it may be to focus primarily on athletics at this stage, this is a grave mistake. Besides meeting academic eligibility requirements, college courses prepare students for careers post sports.

ATHLETES » At this level, it should not be necessary to talk about the importance of putting schoolwork first; you know this or you probably would not have made it this far. You have worked incredibly hard academically to become a student-athlete, so don't let your hard work go to waste by neglecting it now! Just as you should be going into practice mentally present and intentional about your training that day, go into class with a similar mindset. You get out of something what you put into it, so go all in with your classes and you'll be amazed at what you gain!

At this stage, your schoolwork is tailored much more closely to your interests. You will take general credits as well as classes for your major, but there is still a great deal of flexibility in terms of electives, professors, and class times. Make the most of this by exploring classes and interests that will help you grow as a person, explore your passions, and prepare you for the next stage of your life.

Opportunities to learn new things are not just limited to lecture halls and study groups. Take advantage of everything the campus has to offer, whether attending theatrical performances, university orchestra or other concerts, or sporting events on campus. Your free time will be limited because of your own practice and competition schedule, so choose activities wisely, with an eye toward those that best invest in you as an individual.

Some Level 4 athletes may find themselves making the decision to take a leave from school to focus on their athletic career. This usually happens in conjunction with choosing to go pro, although not all athletes who go pro choose to pause their academic studies. This can be a challenging decision. Choosing to go pro may be difficult enough, but choosing to put a pause on your academic studies is every bit as difficult. In 2010, I found myself faced with the opportunity to train at the Olympic Training

Center in Colorado Springs, which meant that I would take leave from college and postpone my studies. Choosing to put my athletic career ahead of my academic endeavors was not an easy decision and one that took a lot of thought.

However, I ultimately decided school would always be there, but the ability to chase my Paralympic dream with everything I had may not. I didn't want to regret not giving it everything I had.

It is important to step back at times and decide what is best for you, and only you can do so. For me, I knew I would be stepping back from my opportunity to experience college in the traditional sense, but I also realized I didn't want to look back and wonder "What if?" when it came to my athletic career. This decision can be very hard for some, while for others it may be a no-brainer, but it is one you should make with the help of your loved ones.

SOCIAL LIFE

An active **SOCIAL LIFE**—the presence, absence, or overindulgence of one—is part of any college experience, and balance is key to keeping it healthy.

ATHLETES >> During the summer before college, think seriously about what you want out of your college experience; this *must* include establishing priorities outside of sports and even academics. The goal, after all, is to become a **COMPLETE ATHLETE**, so consider what avenues you would like to pursue and develop to become a more complete person. These opportunities are going to help you build relationships both with your teammates and friends outside your sport.

You may face new challenges, such as a roommate who does not share your priorities, goals, or schedule. You also may not yet have a network of people to help keep you on track and well-balanced. However, you do have your teammates. You may not know them well yet (you may not even like them all), but they are your new family. It will be worth investing time in building these relationships outside of practice and competition—but don't limit yourself to your teammates as your only group of friends, or you will miss out on the rich diversity college has to offer.

At Level 4, and if you continue on to Level 5, you will realize that there is no cookie-cutter way to approach different aspects of your life, from academics to social life. These are very personal decisions, and we are all different in what helps keep us balanced. What may seem like a distraction to some may be part of a healthy balance for others. It is important to find what works best for you. Some athletes at Level 4 are willing to sacrifice their social life for their athletic performance, and that is what they need to do to perform. Other athletes may realize they need the social life to balance out their athletic career. This is a constant evolution that will take place throughout Levels 4 and 5, and you will constantly step back and evaluate where you are. As you do so, be sure to evaluate where you are not only as an athlete but also as a person. You must maintain balance at all times to be a **COMPLETE ATHLETE**. *Keep in mind that balance can be spread throughout the season. Toward the end of the season when you hunker down, it may feel that there is no balance between your social life and athletic life. However, at the beginning of the season, you may have more time to invest in your social life. Be mindful of where you are and what you need. Keep your priorities in check.*

Sometimes, the best thing you can do when life feels overwhelming is take it day by day and go easy on yourself and your expectations.

ROLE MODEL

No one is ever too old to have **ROLE MODELS**, but at Level 4, it is wise to actively seek real-life role models beyond superstars of the sport. Older players, coaches, trainers, professors, parents, siblings, and friends— anyone who lives the kind of life and holds values consistent with what an athlete aspires to be can stand in this role.

ATHLETES » As discussed above, you will have more eyes on you than ever before. Your conduct as a member of your team affects everyone in your community, from your teammates, coaches, and training staff to your professors and advisors to the alumni network and even the town where your school is located. That school name and those colors are meaningful to many people; respect that and be mindful of the fact you are a role model, whether or not you want to be.

At the same time you find yourself standing as a role model, you should actively pursue positive role models in your own life who can provide feedback and mentorship as you transition into adulthood and pursue your future career and life goals.

JOIN THE CONVERSATION!

Teamwork, respect, and community are all important parts of becoming a **COMPLETE ATHLETE**. Check out the app to learn more!

LIVING YOUR SPORT

For the majority of student-athletes, Level 4 will be the pinnacle of their athletic career. In fact, fewer than 2 percent of student-athletes go pro. For many, this has always been the plan: to pursue sports in college while preparing for a career outside the world of athletics. For others, ending at Level 4 is the result of an injury, not being drafted or selected for a professional team, or a host of other reasons and circumstances. Whatever the case and whether or not athletes seek to move on to Level 5, the way they live their sport at this level will impact their future.

ATHLETES >> You are going to face some heavy decisions regarding whether or not you want to pursue Level 5 and, if so, when to go for it. Whatever you decide, you need to make sure it is the right decision for you, which is why strong knowledge of your foundational values is essential.

Some athletes decide to declare for the draft and leave school early; others decide to wait until after graduation. If you do want to leave early, when do you? Do you leave after a decent season and hope professional teams will believe in your potential? Or do you risk injury and stick around for another year with the goal of having a great season and increasing your prospects? If your goal is international or Olympic-level competition, do you leave school ahead of the Games to devote all your time to training, or do you try to juggle being a full-time student *and* a full-time athlete, realizing there are only so many hours in the day? What about potential career-ending injuries?

Is it worth it to try to fight back to compete again, or is it time to rehab only for the sake of moving on to life outside of sports? Will you always regret it if you never give yourself a shot at going pro, or are you proud of how far your athletic talent has taken you and feel it is now time to move on?

These are the questions only you can answer. Talk things over with your family, trusted friends, and mentors, ultimately, you are the only person who is going to know what feels right to you. The way you live your sport, whether college is the final chapter or merely the next step, is up to you. How are you going to write your story?

1

2

3

4

5

I had only been on my collegiate team for a semester; transferring mid-year meant I came into the season late. However, during spring of my first semester at Gardner-Webb, I made the U.S. National Team and started realizing my potential on the international stage. I knew after comparing the international competition schedule with that of the collegiate schedule, (plus the added support I could receive at home with my family and loved ones) I had a difficult decision to make.

After much thought and plenty of conversations with my family and coaches, I made the decision to close out my semester and return home to Minnesota. I still remember my dad flying out to North Carolina and helping me move out of my dorm. My time at Gardner-Webb, although short, was crucial in finding myself following my injury. As we packed up my dorm room and closed the door on that chapter of my life, I did so with a feeling of peace and certainty regarding the decision I was making. To this day, I have absolutely no regrets about my decision to leave and return home—but I also have no regrets for going.

Ultimately, choosing to go pro was more a decision to return home to my club coach and community. I wanted to put everything I had into chasing my dream of the 2012 Paralympic Games. The financial implications were never a factor in the decision; it purely had to do with my support system and where I saw myself in the future. It wasn't until a few years later I started to receive sponsorships and endorsement deals.

Your collegiate journey may differ greatly from mine, and the decision/opportunity to go pro can also differ greatly. However, I think the most important thing to keep in mind throughout this process is to make the decision that is best for you, whether you close the door on your athletic career following college, go pro, or go pro midway through college. These are some of the most intimate decisions you can make regarding your career, and they shouldn't be driven by social pressures, financial implications, or a desire for fame. Choosing to go professional in your sport is something you can sustain only if you are doing it for the right reasons. Take your time, lean on your support system, and allow yourself to follow your heart.

IN LEVEL 5

You have made it to the top of your sport—now the question is, what are you going to do with that? You probably remember when you once dreamed of making it to where you are today; now it is important to realize, as much as the performance aspect is a part of your career, so is making sure you leave your sport better than you entered it as a Level 1 athlete.

⑤.⑴ ATTITUDE

An athlete almost always goes professional at a young age—as young as the late teen years for gymnasts and some baseball players up through the early 20s for most other sports—with the goal of maintaining a career for as long as possible. This means Level 5 could last 10 years or more, potentially making it the longest segment of an individual's athletic journey.

Because this period can stretch for a number of years and through significant changes (both internally and externally), an athlete must be willing to evolve. Whether dealing with an aging body, maturity that comes from experience, new advances in sports science, new relationships, starting a family, or moving to a new city, state, or even a foreign country, athletes must remain open-minded and adaptable to the major life changes Level 5 can bring. These tools will prove essential for a **COMPLETE ATHLETE**.

RESPECT

RESPECT, in its many facets, is one of the cornerstones of success at Level 5: respect for your team, your community, your coaches, and your sport.

ATHLETES >> As in Level 4, you are representing a team and a tradition bigger than you. When you put on that jersey or don that uniform with the flag of your country, you are standing as an ambassador for everything that symbol represents.

That should simultaneously fill you with pride and humility; it should also give you pause in terms of how you conduct yourself. You have been entrusted with the privilege of being part of that team and all it represents.

Part of your respect for your team is how you give yourself to training, and it is here your respect for your coaches comes into play in a new and exciting way. Now, your relationship with your coaches and your training team will take on a different dynamic, one where you function more as partners and peers. Of course, no matter how old you get, your coach will still be giving directions on what to do and how to train, but since you are no longer a student, the dynamic will shift to one of mutual respect as professionals.

The respect and love for your sport that was such an important part of development in Level 1 will prove just as vital now. As a professional athlete, *you* are the one who has to make the decision every day to keep doing what you do. Your parents aren't there to push you, nor do you have a scholarship keeping you tethered to your school. You may have a contract, but contracts can be broken. Ultimately, every professional athlete will ask at some point in his or her professional career, "Why am I doing this?" The only answer that will bring true satisfaction is not "for a paycheck" or "out of a love for winning." The answer must be pure respect and love for the sport.

My coach, Steve, and I have a unique relationship. As I was growing up, he was one of my first club coaches as well as my elementary school physical education teacher. He then coached my two older sisters throughout high school swimming and coached me during high school as well. Steve and I remained in contact after I graduated, and, in 2014, following a severe arm injury, I started working with Steve again. At that point in my career, Steve and I hadn't worked together since my days as a high school swimmer—before my paralysis. Following my arm injury, I knew I wanted to return to the sport and not be forced into retirement due to the injury, so I reached out to the very coach who instilled the love of the sport in me as a child.

Working with Steve at this point in my career, as I began my journey back from injury and worked toward my second Paralympic Games, was definitely a shift from working with him as a high school athlete. However, I love the dynamic! Because we have known one another so long, there is a tremendous degree of trust. He knows when to push me—when my mind is trying to tell me I'm done but my body really does have more to give in the pool. He also knows when to rein me in because I'm insisting I'm OK even though I'm trying to push through in a way that is counterproductive. On the flip side, he knows he can trust me to let him know when I need to dial back or when I really do have it in me to keep pushing. There is a strong trust and a mutual respect for one another and our roles that makes the relationship so strong.

When I was first paralyzed in 2008, I thought my swimming days were over. A few months after my injury, I was exposed to the Paralympic movement, and within 48 hours of learning about it, I found myself at the pool wanting to try to get back in the water and start swimming again. The idea of returning to the water brought a lot of hope and excitement, but it also brought fear of the unknown. I had been a swimmer my entire childhood. Seeing how much my body had drastically changed in the few months since my injury left me with many questions. But my respect and love for the sport ultimately gave me the courage to face those fears, to trust in the water as a place that for so much of my life had brought solace and clarity.

When I first entered the water, I remember looking up at my coach (at that time) with an expression of uncertainty as to what to do. In that moment, he encouraged me just to begin swimming. Placing one arm in front of the other the same way I had done for years, I looked down toward the black line on the bottom of the pool, and all of my fear and uncertainty washed away. It was just me and the water. Within four or five strokes, I felt at home.

For the next six years, my career seemed unstoppable as I set world records and won Paralympic medals. But then, in 2014, I had a fall that severely injured my left arm and caused nerve damage extending up to my shoulder. Suddenly, I found myself once again unable to move the way I used to, and when I re-entered the water after this injury, I realized I was going to have to fight back from almost zero for a second time. My coach didn't even put the clock on me at first; he didn't want that to discourage me. The focus needed to be on simply getting a feel for my new physical reality. That was when I had to ask myself a very serious question: Was my career built on the fact that I love to win or that I love to swim?

If you've made it to Level 5, you are probably used to winning or at least being a top contender. But if that is all your career is about, what do you do when that changes? What do you do after an injury or after retirement? The moment of winning doesn't last. That is temporary—then you're on to the next match or the next game or the next race. There has to be something that drives you beyond trophies, medals, records, rings, and applause. If not, the day will come when you look back at every sacrifice you made along the way and wonder what it was all for. Competing solely to win isn't enough. You have to rediscover the joy of the sport. That's where you will find meaning in what you do and respect for everything it takes to do it successfully.

SPORTSMANSHIP

Athletes who reach Level 5 are invariably fierce competitors; even people who are easygoing in their personal life have an aggressive side when it comes to their sport. This intensity is the driving force behind the traits that help an athlete reach the highest levels of success: goal setting, determination, and focus. But this intensity can also bring with it some negative traits. **SPORTSMANSHIP** toward one's self, introduced in Level 3, will continue to be incredibly important now as mistakes and losses can seem magnified on the world stage.

ATHLETES >> Your life as a professional athlete will be dictated and, in many respects, controlled by your sport in ways you probably never anticipated. Everything from the timing of certain events to your emotional state after major competitions to the way your successes or failures seem to follow you can take a toll on your mental health. It is extremely important you respect yourself enough to deal with all of these pressures in a healthy and understanding way.

As a Paralympic athlete, my life is dictated by a four-year cycle. In some ways, the predictability is nice because it feels rhythmic and organized; in other ways, it can feel very constricting—most notably during what many Olympians and Paralympians recognize as the "Post-Games Depression."

As the Games approach, there is so much excitement and energy building up as training increases ahead of team trials. Then, once you are actually at the Games and in Olympic Village, the days and time don't even matter anymore; your entire schedule is organized around preliminaries and then races. Everything is about that one moment of competition. Then what? If you win a medal, what does it mean? If you didn't, what does that mean? Does it haunt you? What do you do with your time and energy now? Do you start training for the next Games, or is it time to move on from your career as a professional athlete? During the four year cycle, highs have seemed higher and lows have seemed lower. It finally crescendos with the Games as the end goal. I know this is true for a lot of athletes who are coming off any major, career-capping competition, be it a Super Bowl, Stanley Cup, World Cup, Pan-Am Games, or whatever serves as the pinnacle of your sport's season. Once it is over, you are faced with a lot of questions.

All of the grace, respect, integrity, and understanding you have been working to show your teammates and your broader community for so long all now need to be faced inward. The Post-Games Depression is such a prevalent struggle that sports psychologists help athletes to both prepare for it as well as navigate it when it strikes. In fact, I even planned my wedding to take these blues into account, setting the date for late December 2016, so I would have a full three months to process everything and return to myself before starting my new life with my husband.

The point is, be gentle with yourself as you come out of the bubble. Competition is in our blood; performance is in our DNA. Be sure to show yourself that same sportsmanship you've been trained to show others. If you did well, how are you coping with a return to normal life now that the moment of glory is over? If you didn't, are you reliving those mistakes over and over, letting them affect you in unhealthy ways? Don't be afraid of self-care; don't think talking to a sports psychologist shows weakness. The steps you need to take to bring your emotions back to a healthy and well-balanced state are an extension of sportsmanship. Sportsmanship is, after all, showing respect to your competitor; now, you are extending that respect to your greatest competitor of all—yourself!

JOIN THE CONVERSATION!

Sportsmanship, leadership, and professionalism are all core aspects of becoming a **COMPLETE ATHLETE**. Learn more by downloading the app!

TEAMWORK

A **COMPLETE ATHLETE** who has reached Level 5 understands a team is more than just one star player and that arrogant or selfish athletes quickly lose the respect of teammates. No matter how talented an athlete may be, no one makes it to the professional level without numerous people providing a lot of support behind the scenes. This team-behind-the-team is an extensive network and has consisted of other athletes, coaches, trainers, medical professionals, families, and spouses. Now it may also include agents, sponsors, marketing teams, and even the staff of the facility where an athlete trains, not to mention the fans.

ATHLETES >> Depending on the nature of your sport, you may find yourself training with your teammates every day, or you may workout at a training facility with people who will eventually be your competitors. Some training centers attract athletes from all over the world, which means the person swimming or running in the lane next to you might not even represent your country. The way you treat these fellow athletes will have a major impact on everything from your daily interactions to your reputation within the sport. That doesn't mean you shouldn't be a fierce opponent in every single practice or competition—after all, one way you should respect your fellow athletes is by bringing your A-game every day to push both of you to improve—but the way you treat people off the field, court, track, or mat will affect the stability and support your team offers you in return.

Don't forget to be a good teammate to your team at home, too. Who greets you when you come through the door at night? You need to have personal engagement with more than just the people you train with or your coaches, and your family provides a huge component of your mental and emotional readiness. Whether or not you want it to, your personal life will affect your professional life and performance. Make sure your personal life is not neglected; this is the team that will be in your corner when all else fails.

As I look back at my career and reflect on the highs and lows, I have found my team extends far beyond the members of Team USA. On September 2, 2012, I found myself on day three of competition at the London 2012 Paralympic Games—my first as a member of Team USA. I went into finals that night as an underdog: in fifth place and racing in an outside lane, lane 2. I felt as though I had been counted out by so many people prior to that race, but as I entered the ready room, I knew something inside me was more ready than I had ever been. Waiting for my race to start, I gained strength with each passing moment, almost as if I could feel the strength of my community there with me. As I wheeled out onto the pool deck that evening, there were nearly 18,000 spectators. It was so loud at moments you could barely hear your own thoughts. However, for just a moment, a split second prior to the race, my world went silent. I have since referred to that moment as my moment of clarity. I knew as I stared down at the pool and the black line that I was ready. I sat on the starting blocks and again felt the power of my community behind me as I prepared for what has since become the race of a lifetime.

Just 31.13 seconds later, my hand reached the wall, and I saw one light go off on the starting block at the end of the lane. As I heard my name announced with the words "Paralympic Champion" and "Paralympic Record," I was in complete and utter shock. With each passing moment, those words started to dawn on me, and I realized I had just fulfilled my ultimate dream: to become a Paralympic Gold Medalist.

Later that evening at the medal ceremony, I sat on the podium. To the left in the stands were my Team USA teammates; to the right were my family members. Straight down the pool I saw our flag rise as I heard our national anthem play. In that moment, I realized the medal hanging around my neck had nothing to do with the race —it represented the journey. That medal represented the transition from hoping to believing again. It represented the love and heartbreak. It represented the success and the failures and the sacrifice.

But, above all else, that medal represented a community— the very community that pushed me one step further when I wanted to give up, the community that believed in me when I questioned myself, the community that loved and supported and never doubted. We are only as good as the people we surround ourselves with. If it weren't for the people in my life, I would have never won Paralympic gold.

So as we talk about our teams, as we realize the importance of our communities, we must, as athletes, be humbled by the fact that our greatest moments of success are about so much more than ourselves.

JOIN THE CONVERSATION!

Live your sport & join the **COMPLETE ATHLETE** community of athletes, parents, and coaches by downloading the app today!

PROFESSIONALISM

For professional athletes, their sport is no longer a passion or a hobby—it is a bona fide career. That means there are different pressures and financial implications, but in the midst of that, professional athletes must remember money cannot be the ultimate motivation for competing. A true Level 5 **COMPLETE ATHLETE** has to find the balance between these varying demands and maintaining love for the sport.

ATHLETE >> The mark of **PROFESSIONALISM** in a professional athlete is practicing the sport for reasons other than money. While this may sound contradictory, it does not mean the financial side doesn't matter. Of course it does. This is your career and a major way, if not the primary way, in which you support yourself. So much of what a Level 5 athlete has to take into account is tied to money, from performance bonuses to endorsement deals to contract issues. All of these factors do matter a great deal, but at the end of the day, athletes who compete primarily for money tend to burn out faster because their heart is not in it and the pressures become too much.

After all, so much can affect your career. While injuries are a major consideration, the way reputation can influence contracts and sponsorships is just as serious. From the way you behave in public down to the brands you are photographed using—these can all have financial implications. Sponsors may decide not to renew the partnership or may even decide to cut ties all together if a scandal erupts over your actions or words. There may be clauses that stipulate you will only wear certain brands in public and anything else could be considered an endorsement of a rival brand. For many athletes, it feels like living in a fishbowl: Every move you make, everything you say, every post you make on social media is endlessly scrutinized, dissected, and judged. It is true most professional athletes are not famous, but you never know who will recognize you... and when... and where... and doing what. Many professional athletes find it hard not to buckle under pressure and to always be on their A-game in the public sphere.

One secret of athletes who are most successful at maintaining a solid reputation is a strong sense of community and firm trust in a very close-knit group of friends and family with whom they can let loose, be goofy, vent, and otherwise blow off steam without fear of judgment or scrutiny. By having a safe place to retreat, professional athletes can better navigate the extreme pressures and stresses of life in the spotlight while still maintaining a public face that positively represents their team, their sport, and their own name.

It is crucial you find balance in the professional aspect of your sport. At this level, you are naturally going to feel pulled in many different directions by different people. As a professional athlete, you have individuals who have an invested interest in your career, and your performance may possibly be a metric by which their performance is evaluated as well. However, you must keep a small, tight-knit group of peers, mentors, loved ones, and family members who have your best interest at heart and allow them to serve as your guiding compass.

From a professional standpoint, the process of managing expectations for yourself and others is incredibly difficult as your life and career evolve.

Following the London 2012 Games, I began to explore career passions outside of the water. Two of those passions include speaking and writing. Writing can be done from anywhere, but speaking requires travel. It was important for me to recognize devoting time to traveling to different cities across the country placed an added dynamic on my training schedule. However, the mental and emotional gain in allowing myself to pursue other passions has allowed me to maintain balance in my life as a professional athlete. There are individuals who view a career path outside of athletics as a distraction, but for me, the speaking fuels my athletic performance and helps create a healthy balance.

As you grow in your career, other opportunities may present themselves. When this happens, tune out the outside noise, step back, and evaluate what is best for not only you as an athlete but also you as a person. As I have gotten older, I have learned that to grow and excel as an athlete, I must challenge myself to grow as an individual. Part of being the best version of you is continuing to challenge yourself to become a well-rounded individual. This, in turn, will make you a more **COMPLETE ATHLETE.**

Be mindful of your "why"—why you compete—and where your passions lie. And when you feel the pressure of your growing community, whether from sponsors or fans, allow yourself to view that as added support rather than added expectations.

LEADERSHIP

It is safe to say just about every athlete who makes it to Level 5 has been a leader at some point in his or her career. At this point, an athlete does not necessarily need to work on learning how to lead a team—that was probably learned long ago. Instead, a professional athlete should focus on learning to lead his or her own life. While there are many outside pressures that can influence or try to sway an athlete one way or another, a person with a strong sense of self-leadership will be better equipped to make smart life decisions.

ATHLETES >> You have spent much of your life dreaming of where you are now. It is up to you to make the most of this opportunity. Very few people actually get to live out your reality, and the window in which your body is conditioned right to take the strain of professional training and competition is relatively small, so don't waste this opportunity. Take the lead in your own life as you make both short- and long-term decisions. Only you can determine which sacrifices are worth making and which decisions are best for you and your family, whether choosing to move or retire, change coaches, or try a different training facility. One exciting change at this level is the way your relationship with your coach becomes more a collaboration. Your coach will still take the lead when it comes to training (that is a coach's job after all), but now your relationship is such that you will weigh in and set goals together. If your current coach is not working out or you feel you would do better elsewhere, you may have the option to hire someone else or even ask to be traded.

The point is you are now in a position to take ownership of your life and career as never before. The best way to do this confidently is to trust and lead yourself rather than to allow yourself to be blown around by circumstances or have your life dictated by others' opinions. You've earned this; make the most of it!

 ## PREPARATION

Investing in mental **PREPARATION** as part of your career is every bit as important as physical preparation. This goes beyond mental toughness to mental awareness, where an athlete is invested in his or her own mental health so they enter practice, competition, and

even everyday life refreshed and present in the moment.

ATHLETES >> Physically, you've probably got prep-aration down to a science or else you wouldn't be at Level 5. Mentally, however, it can be a lot harder to figure out exactly what you need emotionally and even spiritually to get yourself in the best possible mindset for maximizing your performance in training and competition. Something as simple as stopping to ask yourself if an extra gym day will benefit you if you aren't mentally present can do a great deal for helping you get the most out of your time.

Whether you work with a sports psychologist, talk to a counselor, meet with a religious advisor, or spend time with a mentor, investing in your mental preparation can help prevent burnout and help you bounce back faster from injury. By preparing yourself for the inevitable and unpredictable twists and turns of an athletic career, you can put yourself in a better state to make small decisions about daily training and large decisions that can affect your future.

FITNESS

As training becomes more intense and contact gets more aggressive, injuries are inevitable. Whether you experience something as relatively small as a rolled ankle or pulled hamstring to something major like a broken bone or concussion, your willingness to rehabilitate the injury properly will prove essential in the healing and recovery process.

ATHLETES >> One of the most frustrating moments of an athlete's career is dealing with the aftermath of an injury. Not only is it maddening to have your performance affected and possibly be pulled from competing, but also incredibly humbling to have to work on such basic skills as range-of-motion exercises or lifting extremely low weights as part of the healing process. As a competitor, the natural tendency is to go all out as quickly as possible, but that can drastically slow the healing process or even lead to re-injury.

Nevertheless, getting back to fundamentals is a major factor in **FITNESS** and will absolutely affect how quickly and effectively you are able to return to your sport. Even injuries that are not catastrophic or carry with them lingering problems like nerve damage can still require maddeningly slow rehabilitation. In these situations, the most valuable thing athletes can do is swallow their pride and not rush the process. If you have a team around you trust, listen to them when they tell you to slow down and work in small increments. There is a fine line between being tenacious and being irresponsible.

In 2014, I suffered a severe injury to my left arm. Unfortunately, I was left with permanent nerve damage. In the early months following my injury, I felt myself spiral into a world of unknowns and uncertainty, and I had more questions than answers. At the forefront of all those emotions was the lingering question: Will I be able to return to the sport I have loved my entire life? If I do return, will I ever be the athlete I once was, or will I be forced into retirement?

Following my paralysis in 2008, I immersed myself in swimming as a way of moving on with my life. In those six years between my two injuries, I spent a total of only a few months out of the water, including the initial months following my paralysis. Six months after my arm injury, I found myself committing to the idea of returning to the pool because I rejected the idea of having to give up based on circumstance rather than choice.

I knew my return wouldn't be easy. I knew my body no longer worked the same way it did months prior. But I also knew the flame that burned inside me, the desire to make a run for my second Paralympic Games, burned so strong that I couldn't give up without a fight. So I fought with the help of my coach, my trainers, my husband, my parents and so many others; I fought every day for a dream because I wasn't ready to say goodbye.

We often talk about athletic comebacks—what it takes to return to competition following devastating injuries —and to me they all include two simple components: the will to never give in and the gift of an incredible community. Returning to competition, expecting yourself to perform better than you ever have following a devastating or even permanently debilitating injury, isn't something any athlete can do alone.

It takes a belief that you can be better, you can fight back, you can defy all odds, and you do not have to be a victim of your circumstance—and that kind of support and encouragement requires a community. A comeback is about the desire to redefine all limitations, having the courage to do what many would call impossible, holding on to the passion for what you love to do, and (most of all) having the grace to know when you simply cannot do it alone.

Making a comeback following injury is possibly one of the hardest challenges an athlete can face. It requires grit, patience, resiliency, and a lot of heart. Upon my return following my arm injury, I had no idea where my career would go. I had to decide if the reason I was still swimming was because of my undying love for the sport or because I loved to win. I knew loving to win simply wouldn't be enough to fight back from an injury like this—I had to be doing it for the deeper love. Each day I woke up and gave my best; that is all any of us can ask of ourselves. Some days that meant I was able to train; other days I was to simply focus on the mental and emotional components of my training. With each passing day, despite the struggle, my coach helped me find that love—a love that wasn't dependent upon performance. Because of that, I was able to show up every day and fight. I knew I owed it to myself to see this dream through, and I had come to terms with the idea that however this journey ended, as long as I gave everything I had, it would be enough.

On July 3, 2016, I sat in a ballroom with my fellow teammates and peers as we waited to hear our names called. Team USA for swimming was named the day after competition concluded at trials, and our family members and coaches were asked to wait outside the ballroom. We waited to hear our names called in alphabetical order. The emotions in that room made the air feel thick, as each name brought either celebration or heartbreak.

Finally they made it to the end of the alphabet and I heard my name called. Everything we had been through, everything we had sacrificed, came together in that moment. As I wheeled out of the ballroom to my coach, future husband, and parents, I had tears in my eyes as I held my Team USA shirt. In an instant, they all began to cry, too. I wheeled toward them and looked at each one, knowing what we had all given, as a group, to make this dream come true.

Sometimes the greatest moments in our career will not come with a medal or records. Sometimes the greatest moments are about looking back and knowing the fight was worth it, about seeing the very people who got us there and realizing you and your team redefined limitations.

You can't mentally prepare for a catastrophic injury; it is impossible to fully understand until you are in the thick of it. If and when it happens, all you can ask of yourself is to put one foot in front of the other and climb back up. On the days when you can't get traction, that is when you lean on your community. You have made it this far. If that flame still burns deep inside you, do not allow an injury to define your athletic fate. Fight back and fight for that dream the young Level 1 athlete inside you dreamed about as a child.

5.4 TECHNIQUE

Even though it sounds too elementary to matter, practicing **TECHNIQUE** needs to be a priority for professional athletes. From changing philosophies on best practices to emerging developments in sports science to adapting to the needs of an aging body, keeping technique at the forefront of training will help an athlete stay on top of his or her game.

ATHLETES » In Level 4, we discussed as a college athlete, you likely had access to more resources than ever. Logically, it would seem this would be even more so at Level 5. Unfortunately, this may not be the case. In a league sport, there will likely be as many, if not more, cutting-edge resources available. An individual sport, however, is a different story.

3

Contrary to popular belief, most professional athletes who compete at the national and international level do not make huge amounts of money. Many work part-time jobs to help provide for their families and pay for their training. If they do not play for a league or live at an Olympic training facility, they must make difficult decisions regarding how to invest a limited amount of money to get the most out of their training. Athletes hoping to go professional must understand this reality before taking the leap. This is also why there has to be a driving motivation other than money.

4

How do you decide which resources carry the most value and which should get priority? How do you maximize your output for the best possible results? These questions can seem daunting. You may think something as basic as technique could be put aside in favor of other aspects of training that seem more important. But it is precisely *because* technique is so basic that it will always be worth the investment. Whether your resources are unlimited or you have to get creative about funding, technique should always be at the top of the list. It may not seem glamorous, but proper technique helped get you where you are, and it will help you stay there. No matter how old you are or how long you have competed, technique matters.

As a Level 5 athlete, technique remains one of the most vital parts of our careers. At this level, we are learning it takes a lot more effort to advance our performance. Our bodies are getting older, and dropping time or mastering a new maneuver becomes harder and harder. One way we can aid ourselves is to change up our habits to give our bodies a restart of sorts. We find ourselves playing with the timing of our practice schedule to find the best time to maximize our training. We play with the amount of sleep we are getting, the best time to go to bed and get up. To improve performance, we mostly focus on a series of small metrics. Just as we adjust our sleep schedule, recovery process, and nutrition, we must also focus on adjustments to our technique.

As our bodies grow and age, we must adapt our technique accordingly so we can be as efficient as possible and also prevent injury. Following my arm injury, I thought I would no longer be able to swim breaststroke due to the loss of function in my arm and the motions and muscles the stroke requires. However, only one month before Paralympic trials, my coach and I were working with another coach on drills to increase my body awareness in the water and fine-tune things as we made our final push. In the process, we realized one of the drills we were doing for other strokes could actually be applied to breaststroke. As a group, we played with it, and before we knew it, we had reinvented my stroke for breaststroke in a way that took pressure off the areas in which I no longer have function and utilized my strengths. As a result, I entered myself in the 100 Breaststroke one week before trials. It became one of my best events at the 2016 Paralympic Games, where I ended up with one of the fastest times of my career.

To challenge our bodies and improve at a sport we have been doing possibly 20 years or more, we must get creative, play with the basics learned at Level 1, and see if we can tweak our technique in a way that makes it more effective for our bodies. Level 5 is not solely about who can be the strongest in order to be the fastest. It is about dissecting all the aspects of training and a willingness to think outside the box and get creative. This is how we will continue to improve our athletic performance.

5.5 LIFESTYLE

Maintaining a healthy balance between your career and your **LIFESTYLE** is one of the most difficult challenges a professional athlete will face. Ironically, sponsors actually understand the demands better than family and friends do at times. To keep from feeling isolated, athletes must constantly reassess their priorities to make sure they are being realistic with their expectations of both themselves and those closest to them.

FAMILY

FAMILY may now take on an expanded meaning, extending beyond an athlete's family of origin, and may now include a spouse or partner and perhaps children. This means your priorities and responsibilities will shift as these dynamics change.

ATHLETES >> Your job is to be an athlete, and this job can appear very self-centered because of the time and focus required for self-care and self-preparation, as well as travel and scheduling demands. While these elements are an essential part of being a professional athlete, a **COMPLETE ATHLETE** understands the importance of giving family his or her very best.

Communication is the key to keeping family members aware of your various obligations and responsibilities. Even when spending time with family, you may find it hard to be 100 percent present because your mind is turning over that day's performance or contemplating the next day's workout. You also have obligations beyond training and competition, including sponsorships and other career pursuits such as writing, public speaking, or coaching. Elite athletes are used to demanding a tremendous amount of energy and performance from themselves and can be devastated when they feel they are not measuring up. Be real with yourself about your personal expectations as well as your family's expectations.

Because our jobs as athletes may not seem like conventional jobs, it can be hard for friends and maybe even family members to fully grasp that every moment, every move we make, is thought out ahead of time and affects our job performance. So often, people seem to believe when an athlete leaves training, he or she is done for the day. What most don't understand is, from the moment we wake up, we are making decisions on how to properly fuel our bodies to be prepared for training. Then, following training, we are focused on how to fuel our bodies to recover.

There is also the mental and physical recovery that takes place throughout the day so we can be prepared for our next training session. And when evening hits, everything is focused on getting our bodies prepared to wake up and do it again the next day. That type of commitment can take a toll on relationships. Often times our families are the only people who understand. However, even they can sometimes have a hard time grasping your commitment—especially during the four-year quad cycle for an Olympic or Paralympic Games.

Unfortunately, to be successful as an athlete, we sometimes will have to organize our world in a fairly self-centered way to prepare our minds and bodies for training. Even then, however, we must find balance and prioritize. I can go three or four months without seeing friends when I am in intense training, but I still see my husband every day. I need to make sure that relationship is given priority over all others. My parents and sisters are also a major priority in my life. While even those closest to me may not be able to appreciate every demand of my time or how fully invested I have to be in my sport, nutrition, preparation, and recovery—especially when close to competition—we have strong communication so they understand my time may be tightly restricted for certain periods, but it is for professional reasons and will only be temporary.

It is important to have that open communication with your family and loved ones because they are a crucial part of your team in your athletic journey. Just as we have days where the process can beat us down, our loved ones have those days as well. Keep in mind we are not the only ones making sacrifices for our careers as professional athletes; our loved ones are, too.

ACADEMICS

While many athletes may begin competing at a professional, national, or international level while still in high school or college, for most, **ACADEMICS** in the traditional sense will not be as much of an issue in Level 5. However, this does not mean studying becomes any less important.

ATHLETES » We expect doctors to stay up-to-date on the latest advances in medicine. We expect teachers to be fully versed in emerging research in their field. We expect lawyers, accountants, engineers, and other professionals to keep tabs on changing cases, rules, and methods that affect the way they do their jobs. Why should an athlete be any different?

Just as important as physical training, mental exercise is part of keeping yourself in peak condition. Invest time in research on various aspects of fitness and sport-specific discussions. If you make it a goal to constantly educate and re-educate yourself on how to get the most out of your workouts, preparation, technique, and recovery, you will find it easier to adapt your methods to the changing demands of your body. After all, you will likely be at Level 5 longer than any other level during your career, which means your body will experience transitions and new needs as it ages. When you commit to lifelong learning, you will develop new skills and grow as a person and as an athlete.

Leading up to the Rio 2016 Games, I became very interested in the nutrition aspect of the sport as I began to be more aware of how my body requires different nutrients at different points in my training. I realized this was an aspect of my preparation that I hadn't previously focused on a great deal. By making small changes and becoming more knowledgeable, I was able to fuel my body efficiently and maximize my physical and mental training. I challenged myself to learn more about nutrition and cooking—not just casual meal preparation, but understanding the process, where the foods come from, and different ways to get needed nutrients in my body to fuel myself. Not only did I gain a new skill set that has proven extremely beneficial to my overall wellness and to helping hone my performance to the finest possible degree, but I also discovered I really love the study of nutrition and the art of cooking, so I gained a new hobby, too!

SOCIAL LIFE

As with any profession, being a Level 5 athlete takes a lot out of an individual. When there are constraints on time, **SOCIAL LIFE** is usually the first thing to be cut. By this point, most athletes will understand the sacrifices involved, but it can be especially challenging when those sacrifices leave an athlete feeling alone or left behind in the natural cycle of life.

ATHLETES >> Most people cannot fully appreciate what it means to be a full-time athlete; they think you spend the whole day at the gym and every weekend at special events and epic parties. Aside from your teammates, most people don't accurately understand the constraints of your schedule, your diet, your sleep needs, your study time, or your obligations to existing sponsors and pressure to secure new ones.

It can be hard, too, to see friends go out and enjoy carefree evenings or experience major life events like a wedding or baby without having to take into account the competition schedule or Olympic/Paralympic timeline. At times like these, when you feel a pull toward a more "normal" life, remind yourself why you are doing all of this. The reason can't be money or fame because you will be gravely disappointed. Only a very, very small percentage of people who fall under the heading "professional athlete" ever achieve a life of enormous paychecks and celebrity status; most live much less flashy lives. Of course, there are great moments and exciting times, but more often than not, the life of a professional athlete is lived behind closed doors, stretching and pushing your body to exhaustion because this is what you have decided you want to do.

When you wake up on Thanksgiving morning and everyone else is sleeping in or making plans to hang out with old friends who are back in town, you still have to get up early to train. Even on your days off, your mind will be on the next day's training or upcoming competition. Is it worth it? If your answer to why you compete is for the right reason, you probably won't mind the sacrifices. Then again, we are all human and will have days when we question our choices. There will be times when you want to skip training, don't want to pass up grabbing drinks with a friend, or would rather stay out late instead of giving your body the recovery time it needs. But, in the end, if you are really doing it for the right reasons, you will find that your motivation to keep working at what you love will prove stronger than the attractions of other pursuits. Understanding that motivation and keeping it in sight always is what makes you a **COMPLETE ATHLETE.**

I have been at Level 5 for many years, and even at this stage, trying to maintain a social life is challenging at times. During my four-year quad, I spend more of my time "dry," meaning I have chosen for performance and recovery reasons not to drink alcohol. (Yes, this includes even a glass of wine with dinner or a casual beer with friends.) I have chosen countless times to stay at home, sitting on the couch and doing recovery treatments because that took priority over meeting up with friends. Life as a professional athlete isn't always easy; it challenges you and sometimes leaves you feeling isolated. However, while you may miss out on parts of your social life, you also have opportunities many may never experience. It is a game of give and take, and it is one that takes an extreme amount of focus and dedication.

Unfortunately, many people will not understand the rigor, but those who do are the ones who matter.

Just as we have discussed numerous times throughout Level 5, remember the importance of forming your tight-knit community because those are the individuals who understand the rigor that is your life. Those are also the ones who will help keep you on track and be there not only throughout this stage of your career but also when it is over.

ROLE MODEL

An athlete can never be too mindful of what the uniform symbolizes or what eyes may be watching. An athlete's team represents so much more than just the competing individual.

ATHLETES >> It is so easy to wear your emotions on your sleeve—and so tempting at times. But it is imperative you remember yourself at Level 1 and become the Level 5 hero you would have liked to meet.

Your decisions and behaviors resonate; they have a ripple effect on your entire community. When you put on that uniform, you represent everyone who supports you. Remember, you can make a lifetime of great decisions—in fact, you can't achieve this level of success and not have done so—and no one may pay much attention, but one wrong decision could very well end up all over the news. All it takes is one poor choice. Even if your sport doesn't have a huge fan base, it and you can suddenly be on everyone's radar—for the wrong reasons. You've worked too hard to tarnish your reputation by a moment of weakness. You owe it to yourself and every set of eyes watching you, to give your best both in competition and everyday life.

The pressures at this level can seem unbearable. After all, we have disappointments just like the next person. But the difference between Level 5 athletes and the next person is we represent something much larger than ourselves. One of my favorite things to do as an athlete is to swim in local club meets. It is a great way to race mid-training, but it is also just a community I love to be around as it continues to remind me why I love the sport so much.

Prior to trials for the 2016 Games, I was competing at a club swim meet in Iowa City. By the time I left, many of the young swimmers on the team that hosted the meet had asked me to sign their bags. Before I knew it, nearly every member of the team left with the words "Dream Big" and my name on their swim bags. I would in no way call myself a famous athlete, but to those young athletes, I represented their ambitions and goals—and that they can come true. In that moment, I represented a community much larger than myself to those young kids. Because of that, I knew as I raced throughout the weekend that I had to keep my emotions in check. I could not get caught up in my feelings after a bad race. (And I had plenty that weekend!)

As long as those kids have those bags with my name and the words "Dream big!" written on them in permanent marker, they will have a reminder of the time they met someone who represented the professional face of their sport. Even if you are not a famous athlete, you can still make a lasting impact on your community.

LIVING YOUR SPORT

By Level 5, athletes have probably been **LIVING THEIR SPORT** in one way or another for the majority of their life.

The community that has grown up around each athlete and helped pave the way will be at its largest now, and the potential for an athlete to have an impact is at its greatest.

ATHLETES » You are where you are now because of countless people who have invested in you, supported you, and helped you develop a respect for your sport along the way. It is now your turn to give back—to put into the community what you took out of it to help build up the next generation of athletes.

Living your sport as a Level 5 **COMPLETE ATHLETE** means encouraging aspiring athletes, mentoring younger athletes, and giving back to your broader community and sport in a variety of ways. Sometimes, high-profile individuals (or those seeking to heighten their profile) will work with a community for the sake of media exposure but have little interest in it when the cameras are off. While they may accomplish some good through their efforts, it is much more satisfying and meaningful to connect with your community because of your personal love for what it represents in your life.

One of the most difficult decisions any athlete will ever face is when to retire. Hopefully, it will be a decision you are allowed to make on your own terms; sometimes, it will be forced upon you due to injuries or other circumstances. Knowing you dedicated such a huge portion of your life and youth to this one thing can often leave athletes questioning whether it was all worth it in the long run. When that day comes, if you have stayed true to your principles and pursued your athletic goals for the right reasons, you can close the door with peace and calmness, knowing you left your sport better than you found it. That is the power that comes with becoming a **COMPLETE ATHLETE**.

JOIN THE CONVERSATION!

For more stories and conversations with athletes and coaches, download the **COMPLETE ATHLETE** app!

MEET THE TEAM

DON YAEGER is a nationally acclaimed motivational speaker, longtime associate editor of *Sports Illustrated*, and author of more than 25 books, 10 of which have become *New York Times* best sellers. Don has written books with Hall of Fame running back Walter Payton, UCLA basketball coach John Wooden, baseball legends John Smoltz and Tug McGraw, and football stars Warrick Dunn and Michael Oher (featured in the movie *The Blind Side*), among others. He teamed with Fox News anchor Brian Kilmeade to pen the 2013 best seller *George Washington's Secret Six*, a look at the citizen spy ring that helped win the Revolutionary War, and then again in 2015 for *Thomas Jefferson and the Tripoli Pirates: The Forgotten War that Changed American History.*

Don left *Sports Illustrated* in 2008 to pursue a motivational speaking career that has allowed him to share stories learned from the greatest winners of our generation. In this capacity, he is able to share lessons from nearly three decades of studying how highly successful athletes and business professionals think, prepare, work, and live in order to consistently achieve greatness both on and off the field.

TIFFANY YECKE BROOKS, PHD is a writer, instructor, and scholar who has worked with Don Yaeger on eight of his 10 best sellers. She has taught writing and literature at Florida State University, Harding University, the University of South Carolina - Beaufort, Abilene Christian University, and McMurry University. She regularly speaks at scholarly conferences and publishes in peer-reviewed journals; she has also delivered keynotes on character and women's leadership.

Tiffany holds a Ph.D. in English from Florida State University, an M.A. from the University of Bristol in England, and a B.A from Harding University.

JOIN THE CONVERSATION!
Download the **COMPLETE ATHLETE** app now.

ACKNOWLEDGMENTS

Thank you to all of you, the greater sports community, for believing in the power of sport and utilizing it to enhance the lives of young athletes. I truly believe as a greater community, whether you be a parent, athlete or coach, you have the power to truly leave an impact and make a difference for so many.

Throughout my own journey, I have had the honor of working with some incredible coaches, two of whom have left a lasting impact on myself. I want to extend a special thank you to Jim Andersen, who coached me from 2008 through 2013, and to Steve Van Dyne, who has coached me since 2014 through present day as we embark on our journey to the 2020 Games. Both of you have shaped me as an athlete, pushed me beyond limits and believed in not only me as an athlete but me as a person as well.

To my parents, I wouldn't be the person that I am today if it weren't for all of your unconditional love and support. Thank you for always believing in me, supporting my dreams, and pushing me to become the person I am today.

To my husband, thank you for being my guiding compass through life. There has been no greater joy then embarking on this journey alongside you. You have supported my every dream and with you by my side I know there are no limits to what we can accomplish.

To Gary Jabara and the rest of the Complete Athlete team, thank you for all your hard work and dedication to bring this project to life. This book wouldn't be possible without the guidance of all of you.

To my greater community—my team behind the team —
thank you for always inspiring me. Every well-wish, cheer,
and message of encouragement has made a difference
to me. I have learned throughout my career you are only
as good as the people you surround yourself with, and I
feel truly blessed to have so many incredible individuals
a part of my community.

As my father told my sisters and I growing up, "You are
the best, you can make a difference, and you can change
the world." Thank you to all of you, the fans, the coaches,
the officials, the supporters, the athletes, and the parents
for utilizing the power of sport to change our world.